BASIC
ECONOMIC PRINCIPLES

TEACHER'S MANUAL

Sanford D. Gordon
Executive Director
New York State Council on Economic Education
Russell Sage College

Alan D. Stafford
Assistant Professor of Economics
Niagara County Community College

GLENCOE

Macmillan/McGraw-Hill

Lake Forest, Illinois   Columbus, Ohio   Mission Hills, California   Peoria, Illinois

Send all inquiries to:
GLENCOE DIVISION
Macmillan/McGraw-Hill
15319 Chatsworth Street
P.O. Box 9609
Mission Hills, CA 91346-9609

ISBN 0-02-819960-X (Student Text)
ISBN 0-02-819970-7 (Teacher's Annotated Edition)

 2 3 4 5 6 7 8 9   92 91

CONTENTS

TEACHER'S MANUAL

INTRODUCTION

Economics, like any subject, can be most successfully taught to students when they recognize what they can gain from the learning. With that in mind, *Basic Economic Principles* has been written to emphasize the relationships between the economic concepts taught in school and the events and challenges that young people experience on a daily basis. *Basic Economic Principles* is designed to reach out to students and draw them into economics. The program makes economics a practical subject, which students can begin to use right now in their own lives.

To motivate students and to make the connection between economic concepts and real-world applications, the concepts taught in *Basic Economic Principles* are introduced with **Personal Narratives**—stories in which the narrator/protagonist is a young person or someone with whom young people can identify. These are not case histories in the common vein. They are dramatically structured narrations that will enable teachers to more easily draw students into discussions of how economic principles have a continual impact on students themselves.

To make economics more accessible to greater numbers of students, the book uses more than one hundred **teaching photographs**, each accompanied by a caption that describes an economic principle using the chapter's vocabulary terms.

In addition to emphasizing student accessibility, *Basic Economic Principles* is also designed to be flexible in meeting the instructor's needs in different teaching situations. Each chapter is divided into short sections that can each be taught separately. This **section-by-section** structure allows teachers to more easily tailor lessons to the needs of individual students.

THE PROGRAM

The *Basic Economic Principles* program includes

- the Student Textbook
- the Teacher's Annotated Edition of the Student Textbook (including this Teacher's Manual)
- the Teacher's Resource Binder
- the Student Activity Book

THE STUDENT TEXTBOOK

The textbook is organized into 4 parts, 15 chapters, and 57 sections.

Parts

Each of the four parts is preceded by a short introduction and followed by a Part Review, which contains a summary of significant economic concepts and a series of exercises and questions that will reinforce student understanding and develop critical-thinking abilities.

Part 1. Understanding the Fundamentals of Economics. In this part students are introduced to the basic concepts and methodology of economics and are given a foundation for the study that follows.

Part 2. Understanding How Individuals and Businesses Make Economic Decisions. This part focuses on microeconomics and the economic decision-making process. Students learn to recognize the basic concepts of capitalism as it functions in our economic system and to understand demand, supply, prices, and the allocation of resources in our economy. This part also describes the basic forms of business organization found in the U.S. economy and examines the decision-making process that businesses use in attempting to maximize profit in perfect and imperfect competition. Finally, this part explains how demand and supply for factors of production determine wage rates, rents, and interest.

Part 3. Understanding the Economy as a Whole. This part provides a macroeconomic overview of how the economy functions and how the government plays a role in the economy. Students are introduced to methods used by economists to measure the performance of our economy and to evaluate the problems of unemployment, inflation, and poverty. Theories of how our economic system works and how it can be controlled are examined. Keynesian economic theory, monetary theory, and supply-side theory are discussed, as well as practical limitations on the effectiveness of each.

Part 4. Understanding International Economics. This part discusses U.S. trade, exchange rates, and problems this country has had with negative balances of trade and payments. The special problems faced by underdeveloped nations are explored. Finally, this part describes the theories, potential, and limitations of alternative economic systems.

Chapters

Individual chapters are preceded by a list of learning Objectives, which identify the central concepts that will be covered in each section of the chapter. Each chapter ends in a Chapter Review, which includes a summary, *What Have You Learned?*, of important economic concepts from the chapter. Concepts in the summaries are organized in the same order as they were introduced in the chapter, making it easy for students to check their un-

derstanding and refer back to the chapter as necessary.

Each chapter summary is followed by a series of activities, which may be assigned as a whole or in parts. Each series includes

- A list of important *Words and Terms* from the chapter
- A vocabulary exercise, *Building Your Vocabulary*, which requires students to demonstrate their understanding of economic terms by placing them in sentences
- A comprehension exercise, *Understanding Economics*, which requires students to explain or use economic concepts in situations similar to those in the chapter
- An application exercise, *Thinking Critically About Economics*, which requires students to use economic concepts in new situations
- A group of *Special Skills Projects* that suggest enrichment activities for more able or interested students

Some activities are most appropriate for students of specific ability levels. The wide range of activities allows teachers to choose those that are best suited to the needs of individual students.

Sections

Chapters are divided into Sections. Each Section presents a limited number of economic concepts and is designed to be completed by most students in one class period or as one homework assignment.

For many reasons, individual teachers may not choose to cover all the economic concepts included in this text. Sections can stand alone to facilitate individualized instruction and to allow teachers to structure their lessons to cover the topics they feel are most significant. More challenging Sections that might not be emphasized for the class as a whole can still be assigned individually to more able students. Also, the ability to use each Section as an independent lesson will help teachers provide work to allow students who have been absent to catch up.

Each Section includes

- A statement of the important terms and concepts that will be presented in the Section

- A *Personal Narrative*, which tells the story of a person in a situation that involves economic concepts of that section. *Personal Narratives* describe events with which students can identify and demonstrate that economic concepts and problems are faced by people similar to students and their friends and relatives

- Textual material that explains and relates the economic concepts that were introduced in the *Personal Narrative*

- A series of *Self-Check* questions that allow students to check their understanding of important points from the Section (and which can also be used by teachers for brief section-by-section evaluation)

- One or two *Applying What You Have Learned* questions, which may be completed for practice or evaluation

Special Features

Three types of special boxed features are integrated in the chapters: *Profiles, Current Issues,* and *Developing Your Economic Skills.*

The nine *Profiles* demonstrate that economists are real people who help make important decisions. Each *Profile* describes an economist's ideas and how those ideas have contributed to the way the world operates. Each *Profile* is positioned in a chapter to correspond to related economic concepts.

One *Current Issues* feature is positioned just before each Chapter Review. These features encourage students to practice critical-thinking skills and to examine the reasons for opposing points of view. Each describes a current issue of economics that concerns young people, providing two lists of arguments that present opposing points of view. After these arguments are considered, students are asked to draw conclusions about the issue and recommend actions that should be taken.

At the end of each chapter is a *Developing Your Economic Skills* feature, which will help students understand and use tables, graphs, and other methods of organizing and presenting economic data. Each of these features identifies a specific skill and gives a step-by-step example of how to apply it.

Vocabulary Treatment

At the beginning of each Section is a statement of the most important terms and concepts that will be covered in the Section. Within the Section, major terms are set in boldface type when they are first discussed. All major terms are listed in the Chapter Review and in the *Glossary*, and in both the terms are cross-referenced to the specific text pages where they first occur.

Appendixes

Features at the end of the text include a discussion of *Careers and Employment Opportunities* and an economics *Glossary*. The *Careers* section shows students how to evaluate their interests and abilities so that they can choose a career that will be rewarding to them as individuals. Fifteen careers are described as examples. Each of these career choices is explained in terms of the nature of the work, necessary training and education, and the job outlook. The intent of these descriptions is not to focus students' attention on specific careers, but to help students recognize some of the factors that should be taken into account in making career choices.

The *Glossary* includes definitions of all the vocabulary terms from the text. Following each term is a cross-reference to the text page on which the term is first introduced.

THE TEACHER'S ANNOTATED EDITION

In addition to the same material that is found in the student's text, the *Teacher's Annotated Edition* contains

- Annotations that will help you make the best use of the text
- The program description you are reading
- Lesson plans, including student behavioral objectives, teaching suggestions, and strategies for each individual section
- Answers for all section, chapter, and part review material of the textbook

Annotations

You will find annotations on almost every page of the *Teacher's Annotated Edition*, positioned to correspond to specific text material. They have been prepared to help you make the best use of the textbook. Each annotation begins with a key word that identifies the type of information or activity that is being suggested. The following key words are used:

- *Discuss.*   Identifies an issue that could be used as the topic for a class discussion
- *Stress.*   Identifies information that is of particular importance or that could be easily misunderstood if not carefully explained
- *Question.*   Identifies an issue that students could be asked to explain or give opinions on
- *Explain.*   Identifies information that students may find more difficult
- *Values.*   Identifies issues that involve conflicting values

- *Note.*   Provides additional information concerning a topic for teachers. This information may be appropriate for some students but too challenging for others

Lesson Plans

The *Teacher's Annotated Edition* includes a suggested lesson plan and teaching strategies for each individual section. These plans identify the economic concepts that the sections are designed to teach, and they suggest methods for teaching and reinforcing student knowledge. Each Lesson Plan includes the following features:

Objectives.   These student behavioral objectives suggest learning outcomes you can expect students to accomplish when they complete each Section.

Preparation Activities.   The first part of this feature suggests a way to introduce the section's primary economic concept(s) to class discussion. The suggestion begins with an aspect of students' lives with which they can all identify, and leads into a connection between that aspect and an economic principle.

The second part of this feature states the economic concept(s) that are demonstrated in the *Personal Narrative* and explains how these also tie in with students' lives.

Teaching Suggestions.   Discussion topics are provided to illustrate specific aspects of economic concepts. In addition, creative teaching strategies are suggested, including

- *Student Surveys.*   Students gather and evaluate information.
- *Interviews.*   Students interview people who have a special need or responsibility within local economies.
- *Values Clarification.*   Students identify values associated with economic issues and suggest answers to economic prob-

lems that would be most acceptable to themselves and to society in general.

- *Simulations.* Students take the roles of individuals who are involved in economic problems.
- *Debates.* Students identify and debate points of view concerning an economic issue.
- *Small Group Activities.* Students are divided into small groups and given specific tasks to accomplish which are related to important economic issues.

Lesson Checkpoint. The Checkpoint provides answers for the *Self-Check* that concludes each text section.

Follow-up Assignments. This section includes answers to the *Applying What You Have Learned* text sections as well as occasional out-of-class assignments.

Section Evaluation. This section provides a reference to the appropriate Self-Check sections in the textbook to specific questions in the textbook's Chapter Review. At the end of each chapter's set of lesson plans is a *Teacher's Bibliography* for the chapter, including references on topics in economics and on additional teaching strategies.

Answer Keys

As noted above, answers for *Self-Check* and *Applying What You Have Learned* are included in each Section-by-Section Lesson Plan. Answers for Chapter and Part Reviews occur at the end of the set of lesson plans for each part or chapter.

THE TEACHER'S RESOURCE BINDER

The *Teacher's Resource Binder* includes a complete testing program and a wide variety of handouts and activities to be used in class or as homework assignments.

Testing Program

The testing materials include a Pretest, Chapter Quiz, Part Tests, a Final Examination, and an Answer Key.

The Pretest covers general knowledge rather than specific economic concepts. Most students should score well on this test, which will help them develop a positive attitude toward economics.

A selection of test items is provided in each Chapter Quiz. Each classification is associated with a specific level of learning. Listed in ascending order of difficulty, the classifications are:

- *Matching.* Students match economic terms with definitions. (simple recognition)
- *True/False.* Students identify statements as being true or false. (simple recognition)
- *Multiple Choice.* Students choose the correct answer out of four possible answers. (multiple recognition)
- *Fill-in-the-Blank.* Students place economic terms in blanks to complete sentences. Lists of the terms are provided to students. (complex recognition)
- *Explanation.* Students answer questions in complete sentences concerning situations from the text, demonstrating their understanding of economic concepts. (complex recall)
- *Application.* Students write a paragraph that answers questions about a situation they have not studied in class. (application)

Questions are provided that test at different learning levels for most important economic concepts. This makes it possible for the teacher to test the whole class for the same concept, while using individualized tests for students with different abilities.

The four Part Tests include questions similar in nature to those of the Chapter Quizzes. Although the questions test for the same information and understanding as the chapter tests, no question is used twice.

Handouts and Transparencies

Several types of materials are provided for promoting class discussion, demonstrating economic principles through game playing, and illustrating concepts visually for the class as a group. These include

- *Illustrated Discussion Promoters.* These are sketches that illustrate economic concepts. They are designed especially for introducing lessons and for reinforcement for lower-level students.

- *Discussion Topics.* These are short handouts that students can review in class or take home overnight, most appropriate for in-class review and reinforcement for lower-level students.

- *Simulations.* The simulations provide students the opportunity to act out situations that illustrate the functioning of major economic concepts. Instructions and the necessary blackline masters are provided.

- *Transparencies.* A transparency is provided for illustration and discussion of each of the 15 *Developing Your Economic Skills* features.

Activities

The activities provide an opportunity for reinforcement and review and for encouraging students to apply economic principles to situations of daily life.

- *Vocabulary Activities.* These are fill-in questions with a vocabulary list, appropriate for reinforcement at all levels.

- *Critical-Thinking and Decision-Making Activities.* These are applications of economic concepts to everyday situations. The situations are personal and student-oriented, appropriate for all levels.

THE STUDENT ACTIVITY BOOK

The *Student Activity Book* provides four types of supplementary student activities for each chapter in the *Student Textbook*. Each activity is designed to help students achieve a specific set of goals and type of understanding. The activities include:

- *Vocabulary Exercise.* These activities will reinforce student knowledge of economic terms and their definitions. Activities include crossword puzzles and other types of word puzzles.

- *Factual Recall.* These quizzes allow students to test their learning of the basic economic concepts included in the chapter.

- *Using Data.* These activities will help students understand and evaluate either tabular or graphic data. Tables and graphs parallel but do not duplicate those in the Student Textbook.

- *Historical Perspective.* These are brief essays that describe a situation from U.S. history that demonstrates one or more economic concepts. The essays show students that economic problems have existed throughout our history. They are followed by a series of questions that encourage students to apply economic concepts to the historical situations, and which may be used to evaluate student learning.

UNDERSTANDING THE FUNDAMENTALS OF ECONOMICS

CHAPTER 1

Life Is Economics (text pages 4–31)

SECTION A. Unlimited Wants and Limited Resources (text pages 8–10)

Objectives (Lesson Focus)

Upon completion of this section, students will be able to:

- Recognize and explain the economic concept of scarcity.
- Explain how scarcity forces people, businesses, and the government to make choices.

Preparation (Instruction: Pre-teaching—Vocabulary or Activity)

1. Discussion Introduce this section by asking students what single item they would like most to have but which they do not currently own. Ask them why they don't own the item and what they could do to acquire one in the future. Lead the discussion into the concept of scarcity.

2. The Personal Narrative The Personal Narrative for Section A demonstrates how people, businesses, and the government face scarcity. Scarcity affects people in the Narrative in a number of ways. For example, the boy does not have enough money to buy new shoes. Joe can't afford better tools. The boy's mother doesn't have money to buy everything she would like for her family. The city can't keep lions in the zoo anymore.

The Narrative describes situations that will help students become aware of the basic economic problem of scarcity. Students should be encouraged to identify examples of scarcity that they face in their own lives.

Teaching Suggestions (Modeling/Guided Practice)

1. Stress the fact that scarcity necessitates choice. We can't have everything we want, so we are forced to choose what we want most. We usually make choices in terms of how we spend our income.

2. Discuss the difference between the types of scarcity faced by people who are rich and by those who are poor. Poor people sometimes have to choose between heating their homes and having enough to eat. Be sure your students are aware that rich people face scarcity too. If they buy an expensive car, they may not be able to build a new swimming pool.

3. Have your students make lists of at least five things they know their local government does not have enough of. These could include police or fire protection, teachers, parks, roads, or snow plows. Combine the individual lists on the chalkboard. Discuss why the local government does not have these things and what would have to be done to acquire them.

Lesson Checkpoint

Text: Self-Check, text page 10
        Answers

1. We can't get everything we want for free.
2. We do not have enough resources to produce enough products to satisfy everyone's wants.

Follow-Up Assignments (Independent Practice/Extension/Homework)

1. Text: Applying What You Have

Learned, text page 10
Answers

a. The person telling the story did not have enough money to buy a new pair of shoes.

b. Joe Rizzo did not have enough money to buy new tools.

c. The brother did not have a car or nice clothes.

d. The man with the suit did not live somewhere with good streets.

e. The city did not have enough money to feed the lions or to fix the roads.

f. The animals in the zoo did not have large cages.

2. Teacher's Resource Binder: Critical Thinking Activity, Chapter 1 (answers in Binder).

Section Evaluation

Self-Check, text page 10
Understanding Economics, question 1 (Chapter 1 Review, text pages 28–30)

SECTION B.   Everyone Pays Opportunity Costs (text pages 11–13)

Objectives   (Lesson Focus)

Upon completion of this section, students will be able to:

- Recognize and explain with examples the concept of opportunity cost.
- Identify trade-offs that take place whenever a choice is made.

Preparation   (Instruction: Pre-teaching— Vocabulary or Activity)

1. Discussion   Introduce this section by asking students to identify several items they would consider buying if they were given money for a birthday present. Ask them to rank the items from the one they would want most to the one they would least desire. If they could only afford to buy the first item, their opportunity cost would be the value they placed on their second choice. Stress the fact that all choices involve opportunity cost.

2. The Personal Narrative   The Personal Narrative for Section B demonstrates the economic concept of opportunity cost. Opportunity cost is the value of a second choice that is given up when a first choice is taken. The subjects in the Personal Narrative make choices that involve trade-offs. For example, the boyfriend chooses to buy gas for his car rather than a pizza for his girlfriend. To afford gas, he had to give up the company of his girlfriend for at least a period of time.

The Narrative describes a situation that will help students become aware of opportunity costs they pay when they make choices. Students should be encouraged to identify examples of opportunity costs they pay in their own lives.

Teaching Suggestions   (Modeling/Guided Practice)

1. Explain the fact that choices are often no better than the information they are based on. If Ted (from the Personal Narrative) had asked his girlfriend about her feelings before he took her to the movie, he would have had more information. What other choices could he have made? How would his opportunity costs have been different?

2. Discuss the opportunity costs paid by young people who choose to join the military. What benefits do these people receive? What costs do they pay? The costs and benefits of reintroducing the military draft could also be discussed in this section.

3. Have students keep a list of their personal spending for a week. For each purchase made, ask students to identify their second choice or opportunity cost.

Lesson Checkpoint

Text: Self-Check, text page 13
Answers

1. A "trade-off" occurs when one thing of value is given up in order to receive something else, usually of greater value.
2. When any choice is made, there is a trade-off. A second choice is given up to take the first choice. The value of the second choice is the opportunity cost.

Follow-up Assignments (Independent Practice/Extension/Homework)

1. Text: Applying What You Have Learned, text page 13
   Answers

   a. She could have stayed home. Her opportunity cost could have been going out with some of her girlfriends or with another boy. She also could have stayed home to do her economics homework.
   b. Ted could have taken his girlfriend to get a pizza and not gone to a movie at all. He could have taken her to a movie she would have liked better. His opportunity cost was related to the value he placed on her goodwill and company.
   c. Ted could have tried to find some other alternative that would have pleased his girlfriend. He could have used half the money for gas and

bought her a hamburger. His opportunity cost may have been related to his desire not to let her "push him around."

2. Have students interview an older person who has returned to school (either to high school or to college). The decision to return to school would involve many special costs for an older person. Such a person could be giving up a job and income, time to be with families, or many other things. Ask students to list the opportunity costs being paid by the individual they interview.

Section Evaluation

Self-Check, text page 13
Understanding Economics, questions 2 and 3 (Chapter 1 Review, text pages 28–30)

SECTION C. From Resources to Products (text pages 14–16)

Objective (Lesson Focus)

Upon completion of this section, students will be able to:

- Recognize and explain with examples each of the factors of production.

Preparation (Instruction: Pre-teaching—Vocabulary or Activity)

1. Discussion Introduce this section by asking students to identify all the things that are needed to bake cookies. Classify each item according to the type of factor of production. The oven, bowl, and cookie sheet are capital. The effort of the cook is labor. Bringing the factors together is entrepreneurship. It is likely that no natural resources will be directly used, but they are necessary. For example, the grain for the flour had to be grown on land that was a natural resource.

2. The Personal Narrative The Personal

Narrative for Section C identifies the factors of production. The subject of the Narrative is a boy who assembles the factors necessary to produce a dog house. Stress the fact that examples of each factor of production are necessary to accomplish production.

The Narrative describes a situation that will help students become aware of how factors of production are used to create the goods and services they use in their own lives.

Teaching Suggestions   (Modeling/Guided Practice)

1. Discuss the fact that labor implies skills and abilities and not just people. Why do many people choose to go to school? The education and training they receive should increase the value of their labor and their future earnings. Wanting to be a lawyer, a doctor, or a scientist is not enough. People must be trained to have these jobs.

2. Have students complete the following simulation. (Blackline masters for money and factor cards can be found in the TRB):

    Choose three or four students to be entrepreneurs. Give each of them $100 of "fake" money to buy factors of production. Give the other students Natural Resource Cards, Labor Cards, or Capital Cards. The task of each entrepreneur is to buy as many factor cards of each type as possible at the lowest possible cost. For each set of three cards, the entrepreneurs can make one product that can be sold for $50. If they make no products, they go out of business and forfeit all of their money.

    All non-entrepreneurs try to get as much money for their factor cards as possible. If they don't sell their cards,

they get nothing. At the end of the simulation, the students may use the money they earned in either profit or from selling factor cards to "buy" some product you supply (whatever reward is appropriate in your school).

3. Have students complete each of the following sentences:
    a. A tree is a natural resource, but lumber is not, because. . .
    b. A hammer and a computer are both capital because. . .
    c. A high school drop-out and a nuclear physicist do not provide the same type of labor because. . .
    d. An entrepreneur is a person who. . .

Lesson Checkpoint

Text: Self-Check, text page 16
        Answers

1. Natural resources are only those resources that have not been changed by human labor. Lumber, for example, is capital, not a natural resource, because it has been changed by human labor.

2. The four factors of production are natural resources, labor, capital, and entrepreneurship.

Follow-up Assignments   (Independent Practice/Extension/Homework)

Text: Applying What You Have Learned, text page 16
        Answers

a. Natural resources were directly used only in terms of space in which to put the dog house. Trees before they were made into lumber, crude oil before it was taken from the ground to make shingles or paint, and iron ore before it was mined to make nails would be examples of natural resources.

b. Labor was provided by both the boy and his neighbor, Ed. The difference in their levels of skill should be pointed out.

c. Capital consisted of the lumber, nails, paint, shingles, and tools that were used to build the dog house. The truck was also capital.

d. Entrepreneurship was provided by the boy when he organized the production of the dog house. He looked up how to build it. He provided the money to pay for its construction. He got his neighbor to provide labor necessary to production.

Section Evaluation

Self-Check, text page 16
Understanding Economics, question 4
  (Chapter 1 Review, text pages 28–30)

SECTION D.   How Economists Use Models (text pages 17–19)

Objectives (Lesson Focus)

Upon completion of this section, students will be able to:

- Explain what models are and to identify common examples of models used in everyday life.
- Explain why it is necessary for economists to use models in their studies of the economy.

Preparation (Instruction: Pre-teaching—Vocabulary or Activity

1. Discussion   Introduce this section by asking students to look at pictures of various people and guess what their personal lives are like. Point out that people do this all the time as they meet new people. Pictures from old school yearbooks can be both humorous and useful.

2. The Personal Narrative   The Personal Narrative for Section D demonstrates how people use models. When the speaker in the Narrative meets someone new, he forms an idea of what they will be like. In a way he uses a model to predict the future. When people form first impressions, they often change them as they gather more information. Economists do the same when they form economic models. Economic models are used to predict the future and are adjusted as additional information becomes available.

The Narrative describes a situation that will help students realize how they form and use models in their own lives.

Teaching Suggestions   (Modeling/Guided Practice)

1. Have students identify the sports team they are most interested in. Ask them to predict how the team will do in the next season of play. Your students could also explain their predictions. These predictions are models. You could point out that people who bet on sporting events are also using models to predict the future.

2. Have your students complete a survey, as follows. Tell students to write each of their ages on a separate sheet of paper, without their names. Collect the papers. Tabulate your students' answers on the board. List the number of students who are 16, 17, or 18 years old. Find out the total number of students there are at your school in your class's grade level. Divide

the number of students in your class into that total. Project the number of students in each age group for the entire grade level by multiplying the factor you have found times the number of students in each age group from your class. Discuss why this is a model. Do your students believe that its results are valid?

For example, if there are 27 students in your class and the total number is 326, the factor would be 326/27 = 12.07:

Age of Students in Your Class		Projection for Entire Grade Level
16 – 5	× 12.07 =	60.35
17 – 18	× 12.07 =	217.26
18 – 3	× 12.07 =	36.21
19 – 1	× 12.07 =	12.07
27		325.89

Lesson Checkpoint

Text: Self-Check, text page 19
Answers

1. Economists must use models because it is impossible to consider every factor that could affect an economic decision.

2. Models do not always result in accurate predictions because they cannot include all factors.

Follow-up Assignments (Independent Practice/Extension/Homework)

Text: Applying What You Have Learned, text page 19
Answer

Students' predictions will vary. You may wish to add other subjects to the list of predictions. Events of local interest to your students can help to develop interest in this activity. Be sure that students' names are on their predictions to reduce the possibility of creative but socially inappropriate predictions.

Section Evaluation

Self-Check, text page 19
Understanding Economics, questions 5 and 6 (Chapter 1 Review, text pages 28–30)

SECTION E. Making Rational Choices (text pages 20–23)

Objectives (Lesson Focus)

Upon completion of this section, students will be able to:

- Recognize and explain the difference between positive and normative statements.
- Explain the meaning of rational choice.

Preparation (Instruction: Pre-teaching— Vocabulary or Activity)

1. Discussion Introduce this section by asking students to list some of the major goals they have set for their own lives. Discuss these goals in class. Why do students feel that their goals are rational choices? Do other students agree? How do different goals reflect different values? How is it possible for a decision to be a rational choice for one person but not for someone else?

2. The Personal Narrative The Personal Narrative for Section E demonstrates how people try to make rational choices. The subject of the Narrative is trying to make a career choice for her future. Her objectives are not the same as those of her mother. She weighs the costs and benefits of various actions and decides to pursue a career in journalism. She believes that the benefits associated with her decision are greater than the costs she must pay.

The Narrative describes a situation that will help students become aware of the choices they have to make in their own lives. Students plan their choices to receive the greatest benefits at the least cost. These choices are rational choices.

Teaching Suggestions (Modeling/Guided Practice)

1. Describe the various historical choices to your students that may or may not have been rational choices. Examples could include the German decision to use hydrogen in the Hindenburg, Russia's decision to sell Alaska to the United States in 1867, or the decision of the Senate not to ratify the Treaty of Versailles after World War I. Discuss why the decisions were made and whether or not they were rational choices.

2. Divide your class into teams of three or four students. Tell them to pretend that their school has received a gift of $5,000 from a local foundation. The money must be used to improve the quality of education in their school. Have each team establish and rank a list of four possible uses for the money. Ask them to explain their choices to the rest of the class. Discuss whether or not they have made rational choices.

Lesson Checkpoint

Text: Self-Check, text page 23
        Answers

   1. Positive statements can either be proven or disproven, but normative statements depend on different people's individual points of view.

   2. Each individual has his or her own values, making an individual's

rational choice relatively easy to achieve. Groups of people often have different values, and so they often do not all agree on what is the rational choice.

Follow-up Assignments (Independent Practice/Extension/Homework)

1. Text: Applying What You Have Learned, text page 23
           Answers

   Mother's positive statement: "Things are different today. . ." [Statement that women today have more choice in determining their life goals.]
   Mother's normative statement: "You could do something really important. . ." [Statement that being a doctor is more important than being a journalist.]
   Daughter's positive statement: "I get A's in English all the time. . ." [Statement that her English grades are demonstrably higher than her math grades.]
   Daughter's normative statement: "I would be happy writing for a living. . ." [Statement of personal values.]

2. Have your students find articles in local newspapers which describe decisions made by local businesses. Ask students to explain what the costs and benefits of each decision was, or will be. Discuss whether or not your students feel each decision was a rational choice.

Section Evaluation

Self-Check, text page 23
Thinking Critically About Economics, question 5 (Chapter 1 Review, text pages 28–30)

SECTION F. Using the Production Possibilities Frontier (text pages 24–26)

Objectives (Lesson Focus)

Upon completion of this section, students will be able to:

- Read and plot values on a graph.
- Read and explain the meaning of a production possibilities frontier.
- Draw a production possibilities frontier from data supplied on a table.

Preparation (Instruction: Pre-teaching— Vocabulary or Activity)

1. Discussion Introduce Section F by reviewing graphing skills described in Developing Your Economic Skills for Chapter 1. Be sure students are aware that the horizontal axis is the *x* axis and the vertical axis is the *y* axis. In plotting ordered pairs, the value of the *x* axis is given first and the *y* axis second.

2. The Personal Narrative The Personal Narrative for Section F demonstrates how trade-offs can be represented on a graph called a production possibilities frontier. The subject of the Narrative must choose what combination of cucumbers and tomatoes to grow with her limited resources. She draws a graph to help her decide what choice to make.

The Narrative describes a situation in which an economic decision is shown through a graphic model. It will help students understand how graphs can be used to help solve economic problems.

Teaching Suggestions (Modeling/Guided Practice)

1. Explain that the graph of a production possibilities frontier is a very simplified model. It does not include price or mention alternative products that could be produced from the resources available. It is intended more to show students how graphs can be used to represent an economic choice than to approximate reality.

2. Have students draw a production possibilities frontier that represents the different combinations of loaves of bread or cookies they could make from a five-pound bag of flour. Each loaf of bread requires 1/2 pound of flour. Each batch of 48 cookies requires one pound of flour. The graph should look like this:

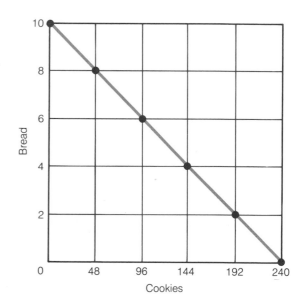

Lesson Checkpoint

Text: Self-Check, text page 26
        Answers

    1. A production possibilities frontier shows different combinations of two products that could be produced from a given quantity of resources.

    2. A production possibilities frontier shows trade-offs as one moves from one point on the frontier to another. A quantity of one product is given up in order to produce a greater quantity of the other.

Follow-Up Assignments   (Independent Practice/Extension/Homework)

Text: Applying What You Have Learned, text page 26
Answers

  a. true

  b. true

  c. false

  d. false

  e. true

Section Evaluation

Self-Check, text page 26
Understanding Economics, question 7
  (Chapter 1 Review, text pages 28–30)

ADDITIONAL MATERIALS FOR CHAPTER 1

Chapter Evaluation
Teacher's Resource Binder: Chapter 1 Quiz

Reteaching and Extension
See the *Teacher's Resource Binder* and the *Student Activity Guide* for additional handouts and activities for Chapter 1.

TEACHER'S BIBLIOGRAPHY FOR CHAPTER 1

Economics Sources

Blaugh, Mark. *The Methodology of Economics: or How Economists Explain.* New York: Cambridge University Press, 1980. An examination of research tools and their uses in analyzing economic problems.

Canterbury, E. Ray. *The Making of Economics.* Belmont, Calif.: Wadsworth Publishing Co., 1976. Explores the evolution of the discipline to the present.

Fusfeld, Daniel R. *The Age of the Economist,* 5th ed. Glenview, Ill.: Scott Foresman and Co., 1986. A popular review of economic ideas.

Heilbroner, Robert. *The Worldly Philosophers.* New York: Simon and Schuster, 1981. A popular review of economic ideas and the personal lives of economic thinkers.

References for Additional Teaching Strategies

Morton, John, et al. *High School Economics Courses.* New York: Joint Council on Economic Education, 1985. New York: 1985. See Lesson 1, pp. 22–26.

CHAPTER 1 REVIEW ANSWERS

Building Your Vocabulary   (text page 29)

1. opportunity cost
2. scarcity
3. economics
4. positive statement
5. natural resources
6. production
7. factors of production
8. production possibilities frontier
9. labor
10. normative statement
11. entrepreneurship
12. rational choice
13. capital
14. model
15. trade-off
16. goods
17. services
18. resources

Understanding Economics   (text pages 29–30)

1. a. There is no limit to what people want.
   b. There is a limit to our ability to produce goods and services to satisfy these wants.

2. John's opportunity cost would be the value he placed on the new shirt that he did not buy.

3. When people make trade-offs, they are trying to maximize their satisfaction. In doing this they try to make rational choices such that their benefits exceed their costs.

4. a. A natural resource would be the tree.
   b. The Indians' efforts would be the labor.
   c. The tools the Indians used would be the capital.
   d. The orders given by the chief would be the entrepreneurship.

5. Models are representations of reality used by economists to simplify economic problems so that they can be more easily understood. They are also used as the basis of predictions of the future.

6. Predictions made by economists are important because they are often used by the government and businesses as the basis for their decisions.

7. The firm would have to give up the production of 50 chairs to make ten more tables.

8. Rational choice is making decisions such that the value of the results exceeds the value of the costs.

9. A positive statement is a statement of fact that can be either proven or disproven. A normative statement involves a value judgment that can neither be proven nor disproven.

Thinking Critically About Economics   (text page 30)

1. The student's list of five items should be clearly explained in relation to why these items are of greater value than alternatives that could have been taken.

2. The student's list of the factors of production should be clearly defined. The distinction between capital and natural resources will probably give students the greatest difficulty.

3. The students' opportunity cost should clearly be the value they associated with their second choice that they gave up when they took their first choice.

4. Other models your students might use could be maps of bus routes or subways, diagrams of how products they buy must be put together, or play plans for football teams.

5. Be sure that all statements identified as positive can be either proven or disproven.

6. The point of this question was to evaluate the students' understanding of rational choice. Look for a clear distinction between the students' description of the costs and benefits of the decision that was made.

7.

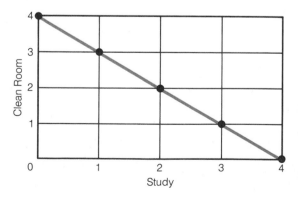

Special Skills Projects (text page 30)

1. The answers of the students are likely to deal more with personal gratification than those of their parents. This can be used as a lead into a discussion of how our needs change as we grow older.

2. The bulletin board can be a good idea for students who want to do something extra but do not have a great deal of academic ability. Try to help them find a different way of expressing the idea of the combination of the four factors of production to make goods and services than the one that was provided in the text.

3. These can be quite useful as the topic of discussion. Encourage students to find opposing opinions concerning local issues. Ask them about the personal values reflected in these opinions. Why do different people interpret the meaning of the same facts in different ways?

CHAPTER 2

Economic Systems: Who Made the Rules? (text pages 32–59)

SECTION A. How Economic Systems Developed (text pages 35–39)

Objectives (Lesson Focus)

Upon completion of this section, students will be able to:

- Explain the basic functions of economic systems.

- Recognize and explain the central characteristics of capitalism.

- Recognize and explain the economic advantages offered by the division of labor and specialization.

- Recognize and explain the relationship between the accumulation of wealth and increased productivity.

Preparation (Instruction: Pre-teaching—Vocabulary or Activity)

1. Discussion Introduce this section by asking students to list five things they own which they feel they could make for themselves *from basic raw materials* if they had to. They may find this list difficult to complete. Then ask them to list five items they own that they could not make. What characteristics can they find that are common to each group of items? Do the items in the second group require specialized tools or labor to produce?

2. The Personal Narrative The Personal Narrative in Section A describes the development of a fictional economic system at the dawn of history. The subject of the Narrative is a native who has the idea of creating a division of labor. His idea succeeds and allows specialization, greater productivity, and the accumulation of wealth.

The Narrative describes a situation that will help students become aware of the function of an economic system in organizing production. It shows examples of the division of labor which can be related to situations that exist in students' lives. Something as simple as having a different teacher with different training for each subject can make this point.

Teaching Suggestions (Modeling/Guided Practice)

1. Try the following simulation: Choose a team of three students. Have them sit at a table with paper, three staplers, three pairs of scissors, and three felt-tip pens. Tell them they are going to manufacture

counting books for first-grade students. They are to fold the paper into fourths, cut it along the folds into four pieces, staple the pages together, and number them from 1 through 8 (one number on each side of each piece of paper). Inform the students that you will not accept inferior or incomplete products. Have your students work individually the first time. Give them four minutes and count their total production.

Discuss how a division of labor could allow them to specialize and increase their production. If one person cuts paper, a second staples, and a third writes numbers, they should be able to produce more books. Try this and see what happens to the number of books they can make in four minutes.

2. Discuss why some people are better at some jobs than others. Are there jobs where it is better to be small? Think of racing jockeys, or a person who assembles electrical components. What types of jobs require strength, special training, or a specialized education? You could lead this discussion into the subject of career choice.

3. The division of labor in a hospital is usually very clear. Either have one of your students interview a nurse, or invite a nurse to speak to your class. Discuss how and why labor is divided in a hospital. What jobs are aids, nurses, and doctors allowed to do? What is the reason for this particular division of labor? What is the "product" a hospital produces? Why is it more difficult to measure the productivity of a hospital than that of a normal business?

Lesson Checkpoint

Text: Self-Check, text page 39
        Answers

1. An economic system is a set of rules that governs what goods and services to produce, how to produce them, and for whom they are meant.

2. The division of labor allows specialization of both labor and capital.

3. An economic system must provide wealth in order to grow.

Follow-up Assignments   (Independent Practice/Extension/Homework)

1. Text: Applying What You Have Learned, text page 39
           Answer

   Three examples of the division of labor include all of the village's hunting done by Grug, all of the fishing by Thump, and all of the bread making by Sluf. This division of labor gave the villagers the time to invest in tools that increased their productivity as well as enabling them to have more time to consider options such as trading with other villages, a possible benefit to enhance their lifestyle and to exchange different skills.

2. Teacher's Resource Binder: Critical Thinking Activity, Chapter 2 (answers in Binder).

Section Evaluation

Self-Check, text page 39
Understanding Economics, questions 1–3 (Chapter 2 Review, text pages 52–54)

SECTION B.   The Basic Questions: *What, How,* and *For Whom*? (text pages 40–43)

Objectives (Lesson Focus)

Upon completion of this section, students will be able to:

- Recognize the three basic economic questions, *what*, *how*, and *for whom*.
- Explain how the three basic economic questions are answered in capitalism.

Preparation (Instruction: Pre-teaching—Vocabulary or Activity)

1. Discussion   Introduce this section by asking students to identify five personal items their parents (of the same sex) buy that they would not want to buy. Hair coloring, false teeth powder, or arch-supports could be some examples. What would happen to a store that wanted to sell to young people but only offered these products for sale? The students could also make a list of items they would buy that their parents would not. Point out that stores must offer products their customers are willing to buy if they intend to succeed. This is the way the question *What* is answered in a market economy.

2. The Personal Narrative   The Personal Narrative for Section B provides an example of how each of the three basic economic questions—*what*, *how*, and *for whom* is answered in a market economy. The subjects of the Narrative are students and their teacher who meet to discuss the management of a school store. They are concerned over its losses and suggest ways to improve its performance. The idea of offering different products that would sell better is suggested. They discuss how to store the new products. Finally, the question of their compensation is discussed. The teacher makes the point that if they are not able to sell more products, they will either have to take a cut in their pay or close down.

The Narrative demonstrates a situation that will help students realize how people like themselves make basic economic decisions.

Teaching Suggestions   (Modeling/Guided Practice)

1. Discuss why many sports stars receive very high salaries. What do they do that justifies earnings in excess of a million dollars a year? How do their earnings help answer the question *for whom*. Remember that it is the people who pay for tickets or buy the products advertised on television that are really paying the salaries. Many people who earn little money cannot afford to go to a game. Do your students feel it would be a good idea for the government to limit what a sports star earns to two or three hundred thousand dollars a year and then force ticket prices to be lowered? In what way would such a law change the way the question *for whom* is answered?

2. Give your students a copy of Discussion Topic 1 from the *Teacher's Resource Binder*. Ask them to describe what the news story shows about the way the basic economic questions *how* and *for whom* are answered in the United States.

Lesson Checkpoint

Text: Self-Check, text page 43
    Answers

1. *What* refers to the decision of which goods to produce; *how* refers to the method used to produce them.

2. In a market system, benefits are allocated according to the value of a person's contribution to production.

Follow-up Assignments   (Independent Practice/Extension/Homework)

Text: Applying What You Have Learned,
         text page 43
         Answers

What?	1. "We should sell candy bars and potato chips."
	2. "How about granola bars?" (There are several other possible answers in the story.)
How?	1. "There's an old one in the basement you could use."
	2. ". . . you could have fewer clerks."
For Whom?	1. ". . . we have been paying clerks $4.50 an hour and haven't earned enough money to cover their wages."
	2. "You could take a cut in pay to, say, $3.50 an hour. . . ."

Section Evaluation

Self-Check, text page 43
Understanding Economics, question 4
   (Chapter 2 Review, text pages 52–54)

SECTION C.   The Role of Profits in the Economy (text pages 44–46)

Objectives   (Lesson Focus)

Upon completion of this section, students will be able to:

- Explain what a firm in capitalism must do to earn profits.
- Explain the relationship between profits and the allocation of resources in capitalism.

Preparation   (Instruction: Pre-teaching—Vocabulary or Activity)

1. Discussion   Introduce this section by discussing specific local businesses that have grown. What is it about these firms that have enabled them to acquire the resources necessary to expand? What is the relationship between their ability to earn a profit and their ability to grow? The same idea can be used for firms that have not grown. Do these firms share low profitability? Is their market saturated with many producers?

2. The Personal Narrative   The Personal Narrative for Section C demonstrates how a person is motivated to go into business by the expectation of profit, and how profits are related to the allocation of resources. The subject of the Narrative is a young woman who is opening a small restaurant on a dock. She believes that retired people who live near the dock will buy her food and make her business profitable. She expects to be able to open similar businesses on other docks in the future. Whether she is able to acquire the necessary resources depends on the success of her first restaurant.

The Narrative describes a situation that will help students appreciate the relationship between a firm's profitability and its ability to afford additional resources.

Teaching Suggestions   (Modeling/Guided Practice)

1. Discuss how much profit is "too much" profit. Few people would complain about a firm making a profit of five to ten percent on its investment. More people would be upset about a firm making a 50 percent return or more. If a firm makes large profits, its customers must be willing to pay its price. Does this fact justify large profits? If not, *how* do your students feel profits should be limited?

2. Many resources are allocated in the United States according to rules set by the government rather than according to

profit. For example, the government has paid farmers not to grow crops. States have allocated inexpensive hydroelectric power to some firms but not to others. Government rules have required firms to hire minorities, or set wage rates that firms must pay. Have students make a list of examples of such rules. Ask them to explain why each rule was established and whether each rule seems to be accomplishing its objectives.

3. The price of fresh produce in grocery stores fluctuates widely. Assign a student to interview a produce manager about his store's pricing policy. How do they set prices? What do they do if there is a shortage of lettuce or carrots? How do they limit losses from spoilage? How do they know how much of each item to order? To what extent is the individual manager responsible for profit in his/her department? If the produce department is profitable, will it be expanded? Why or why not?

Lesson Checkpoint

Text: Self-Check, text page 46
Answers

   1. To earn a profit, a firm must sell products that customers want at prices they are willing to pay.
   2. Profit is the basic method of allocation in capitalism.

Follow-up Assignments   (Independent Practice/Extension/Homework)

Text: Applying What You Have Learned, text page 46
Answers

   a. Regina used natural resources indirectly. The lumber and paint she used were capital but they came from trees and crude oil that were natural resources.

   b. Regina used her own labor for the most part. If she hired plumbers or electricians, their labor could be included.
   c. Regina used the building, tools, kitchen equipment, and the dock itself as capital for her business.
   d. Regina's decision and direction of the other factors of production represented entrepreneurship in this case.

Section Evaluation

Self-Check, text page 46
Understanding Economics, questions 5 and 6 (Chapter 2 Review, text pages 52–54)

SECTION D.   Economic Decisions in Other Systems (text pages 47–50)

Objectives   (Lesson Focus)

Upon completion of this section, students will be able to:

- Recognize and explain the different characteristics of a command economy relative to capitalism.
- Describe how the three basic economic decisions are made in command economies.
- Explain the allocation of resources in a command economy as compared to their allocation in capitalism.

Preparation   (Instruction: Pre-teaching—Vocabulary or Activity)

1. Discussion   Introduce this section by asking each student to write a brief description of what they would look for in a car they would someday like to own. Ask them how they would feel if they could only choose one type of car and if they might have to wait up to two years to get one. This is essentially the situation in many command economies.

Governments in these nations determine what products will be produced. They may choose to produce only one type of car. Also point out that resources are allocated in command economies according to government plans rather than profits which result from consumer demand.

2. The Personal Narrative The Personal Narrative for Section D shows how economic decisions are made in command economies. The subject of the Narrative is a young man who is related to people who live in the Soviet Union. He is surprised to learn about the limitations on their freedom to make economic choices. His uncle explains some of the costs and benefits of command economies.

The narrative will help students become aware of alternative methods of answering the basic economic questions of *what, how,* and *for whom*.

Teaching Suggestions (Modeling/Guided Practice)

1. Divide your class into pairs of students. Tell students to choose and rank the four items they would like most from the list below. Each student should write this list on a piece of paper without revealing it to their partner. On a second piece of paper they should guess what four items their partner chose and what rank each item was given. When the students have completed these tasks, have them exchange their rankings and evaluate the results. How accurate were they in guessing each other's wants?

   This exercise is a much smaller version of the problem faced by planning agencies in command economies. These systems attempt to decide what products should be manufactured. Their people

do not make the basic economic decision *what*. Help your students draw conclusions about the difficulty of planning in such systems.

Items from which to choose:

a. a new bicycle

b. a portable TV

c. a desk lamp

d. a new jacket

e. a new shirt or blouse

f. a new pair of shoes

g. a new watch

h. a typewriter

i. a portable tape recorder

j. dinner at a nice restaurant

2. Write directions for completing a simple task on a paper. Ask a student to read it silently. The student should then go to a corner of the room and whisper the instructions to another student. Do this several times. Have the last student write the directions on a piece of paper. Compare the first and last set of directions. They are likely to be quite different. Discuss how this exercise points out the difficulty command economies have in putting plans into effect.

3. Discuss the fact that schools are much like small command economies. Education is being produced by allocating resources. One job that administrators have is to be sure that all resources (students and other educational materials) are in the right place at the right time. How well does this work in your school? Are students always scheduled into the correct classes? Once scheduling is completed, do all students and other educational materials combine to produce education? Is society getting its money's worth? What difficulties does this demonstrate about command economies?

Lesson Checkpoint

Text: Self-Check, text page 50
         Answers

1. In a command economy, the questions *what*, *how*, and *for whom* are answered by the government.

2. Advocates of a command economy believe that running businesses to earn profit results in production of goods intended solely for the rich, thereby ignoring the poor and unfairly distributing the nation's wealth.

Follow-up Assignments   (Independent Practice/Extension/Homework)

Text: Applying What You Have Learned, text page 50
         Answers

a. A capitalistic firm that makes a shirt no one wants would have low sales and would probably go out of business.

b. A capitalistic firm that hires too many workers would have high costs of production and therefore low profits. It would likely lose money and be forced out of business.

c. A capitalistic firm that makes poor quality goods would soon find that it has no customers. People would buy from other producers of quality products.

d. A capitalistic firm that pays its workers too little would not be able to attract workers and would either produce little or low-quality products that would force it out of business.

    If a firm in a command economy did these same things there would be little effect on the firm. If there were no competition, out-of-style shirts could sell even if they were of low quality. Also, workers would have little choice in where they worked, regardless of the wages. This would mean that inefficient firms could continue to operate and there would be little way to measure how efficient or inefficient they were.

Section Evaluation

Self-Check, text page 50
Understanding Economics, question 7 (Chapter 2 Review, text pages 52–54)

ADDITIONAL MATERIALS FOR CHAPTER 2

Chapter Evaluation

Teacher's Resource Binder: Chapter 2 Quiz

Reteaching and Extension

See the *Teacher's Resource Binder* and the *Student Activity Guide* for additional handouts and activities for Chapter 2.

TEACHER'S BIBLIOGRAPHY FOR CHAPTER 2

Economics Sources

Hacker, Andrew. *Free Enterprise in America*. San Diego: Harcourt Brace Jovanovich, 1977. Written for secondary school students, this book provides an easily understood explanation of the market system.

Lunt, Steven D. *Free Enterprise in America*. New York: Watts, 1985. A short book that explains in simple terms how the American economic system works.

Silk, Leonard. *Economics in Plain English*, revised. New York: Touchstone, 1986. Discusses the basics of an economic system.

Written by a well-known economist and journalist.

References for Additional Teaching Strategies

Dawson, George G. *Free Enterprise in America: Teaching Guide*. San Diego: Harcourt Brace Jovanovich, 1977. While this is keyed to the book by Andrew Hacker mentioned above, it may be used alone for the many excellent activities suggested.

Morton, John, et al. *High School Economics Courses*. New York: Joint Council on Economic Education, 1985. See Chapter 2 for strategies and student handouts on "Different Means of Organizing an Economy."

CHAPTER 2 REVIEW ANSWERS

Building Your Vocabulary   (text page 53)

1. division of labor
2. economic system
3. *for whom?*
4. specialized capital
5. command economy
6. *what?*
7. wealth
8. *how?*
9. capitalism
10. specialization
11. allocation of resources
12. profit
13. traditional economy

Understanding Economics   (text page 53)

1. An economic system is a set of rules that governs how the factors of production will be used to produce goods and services and also determines how these goods and services will be distributed.

2. The division of labor is cutting up the job of production into various parts. This allows specialization in that different individuals can learn how to do each part more efficiently. This also allows for the creation of specialized tools that will add to the efficiency of production.

3. Specialized tools increase the efficiency of production. Greater production increases the ability of an economic system to satisfy needs for current consumption and have production left over that can be accumulated as wealth.

4. There are many examples that could be used for this question.

   a. The question *what* should be answered through the purchase of some item or service.

   b. The question *how* should be answered in terms of cutting cost to improve profitability.

   c. The question *for whom* should be answered in terms of income being dependent on the value of a person's contribution to production.

5. To be profitable, a capitalistic firm must offer products or services that people want at prices they are willing and able to pay.

6. In capitalism, firms that are most efficient should be most profitable. Firms that are profitable will be able to afford more resources. Therefore, resources should be allocated to the most efficient firms in capitalism.

7. a. In command economies, the products that are manufactured are determined by the government.

   b. In command economies, the method of production is determined by the government.

c. In command economies, the distribution of what is produced is determined by the government.

Thinking Critically About Economics   (text pages 53–54)

1. Most of the answers that would be acceptable for this question deal with the greater ability of large schools to serve the diverse needs of many students. Possible answers would include:

   a. ability to afford more science equipment

   b. ability to afford different types of teachers

   c. ability to offer different subjects

   d. ability to afford more tools and machines in shops, etc.

   e. ability to provide more varied points of view

2. The small stores will probably not stock as many specialized items. The reason has to do with turning over inventory. It does not provide as much variety, since it would be poor business to have money tied up in items that do not sell. There is also the possibility of spoilage. It also uses resources and space that could be put to better use.

3. There will be many different salaries offered. Try to draw a correlation between the amount of the salaries and the value of what the worker will contribute to production.

4. There are many possible answers to this question. Try to make it clear that the firm was not answering the questions of *what* or *how* effectively and efficiently.

5. Again, there are many possible answers to this question. Try to show how these firms were more effective and efficient in

answering the questions of *what* and *how*.

6. Owners of capitalistic firms in the United States are allowed to

   a. set their own price.

   b. decide what products to make.

   c. decide who to buy from.

   d. decide what to invest in.

   e. decide what to pay workers.

   f. decide how to make their products.

   (There are many other answers that would be just as correct.)

Special Skills Projects   (text page 54)

1. There will be many variations on this story. All stories should emphasize the advantages offered by this specialized tool and how it contributed to the efficiency of production and therefore to the accumulation of wealth.

2. Acceptable locations should consider potential demand for the product and cost of renting or building in that location. Consideration should be given for the thoroughness of each student's effort.

3. The results of these interviews will vary widely. You could draw relationships between the economic conditions the people live in and their perception of the role of the government in their lives. Do extremely poor people feel the same way as those who are not poor?

PART 1 REVIEW ANSWERS

Understanding Economic Concepts   (text pages 56–57)

1. The answer is provided as an example in the text.

2. When we choose to buy the product we want most, we pay an *opportunity cost*, which is the value of the second choice we gave up.

3. The *four factors of production* economists have identified, which are necessary to create goods and services, are: *natural resources*, things in their natural state that have not been changed by people; *labor*, human effort that is applied to natural resources; *capital*, the tools used by labor in making products; and *entrepreneurship*, the organization necessary to bring about production.

4. Economists use *models*, which are theories of how something works, to better understand the past or present and to predict the future.

5. Economists try to make *rational choices* in which they take things of greater value than those which are given up.

6. Economic systems increase the efficiency of production through the *division of labor*, which breaks the process of production into specific tasks and allows *specialization* in which individual workers concentrate their efforts on one specific task. This enables them to become more efficient at their work.

7. All economic systems must answer the four basic economic questions: *What* (what goods and services should be produced?); *How* (how should these goods and services be produced?); *For Whom* (for whom should these goods and services be produced?).

8. The economic system in the United States is mixed, but it is most like *capitalism*. In capitalism the means of production (factors of production) are owned and controlled by individuals or groups.

9. In capitalism firms that are most profitable are best able to purchase additional resources. Therefore, resources are *allocated* to firms according to the *profits* they earn.

10. In a *command economy*, like the one found in the Soviet Union, the means of production are owned and controlled by the government. This means that most basic economic decisions are made by the government.

Writing About Economics   (text page 57)

1. Students should show an understanding that because of *scarcity* they cannot both buy the supplies they need for their math class and go to a movie. This scarcity will require them to pay an *opportunity cost* when they give up their second choice by taking their first choice.

2. Students should show an understanding that producing and selling letter boxes will require each of the *four factors of production*. The lumber they use was originally a *natural resource* when it was a tree standing in a forest. The student's efforts to make and sell the boxes is *labor*. The hammer and nails they use to put the pieces of wood together are *capital*. Their decision to produce and sell the boxes is *entrepreneurship*.

3. Students should show an understanding that the decision to work together on one job at a time will result in a *division of labor* in which each person will *specialize* in accomplishing one task that is a part of the entire job. This should allow each individual to become more efficient at that task and improve efficiency.

4. Students should show an understanding of the way the three basic economic questions are demonstrated by the problems they have running their appliance store. The good sales of radios and TV's will help them answer the question *What*

they should sell. Hiring a repair person to fix appliances answers the question *How*. Deciding to give, or not give, their employees an increase in salary answers the question *For Whom*.

Discussing Economics   (text pages 57–58)

1. Students should identify the issue that the proposal is based on: Is the rationing plan a fair and efficient way to distribute a limited (scarce) supply of gasoline? Students should clearly state whether or not they support the plan for rationing gasoline. They should clearly explain the costs and benefits associated with the plan and explain why their answer is best.

2. Students should identify the issue that the zoning law is based on: Is it fair to limit housing in an area to those people who can afford to buy and build on a one-acre lot? Students should clearly state whether or not they support the law. They should clearly explain the costs and benefits associated with the law and explain why their answer is best.

Problem-Solving in Economics

Chapter 1   (text pages 58–59)

1. Students should clearly describe the problem and the choice that was made, identify the scarce resources that were used, and describe an alternative use of scarce resources. This exercise may be used to demonstrate the economic concepts of *scarcity* and *opportunity cost*.

2. Students should clearly describe each of their four decisions and the alternative choices they could have made, which were the *opportunity costs* they paid in each case.

3. Students should demonstrate an understanding of the factors of production. Be careful with their identification of natural resources. Students often identify things that have been changed by human effort (capital) as natural resources.

4. a. *Positive*—the population of the U.S. in 1985 is a measurable fact.
   b. *Positive*—the unemployment rate in West Virginia and the rest of the U.S. at any given time are measurable facts.
   c. *Normative*—whether the President of the United States is the most powerful person in the world is a matter of one's individual point of view.
   d. *Normative*—whether watching TV is a waste of time is a matter of one's individual point of view.
   e. *Positive*—changes in the price of products are measurable facts.
   f. *Normative*—whether buying Japanese cars is wrong is a matter of one's individual point of view.

5. The table shows that drivers between the ages 18 and 21 had the highest rate (31.50 per 100,000 drivers) of fatal accidents involving intoxicated drivers in 1983.

   Lists of assumptions could include: young people don't know when to stop drinking; young people aren't as experienced drivers; young people get drunk more often than older drivers; young people are not as responsible as older drivers.

   Students should demonstrate that they have considered the logic of the assumptions on their list. They should

show that they understand the table and that the assumptions are forms of *models*.

6. Students should clearly demonstrate an understanding of *rational choice* by listing and evaluating the costs and benefits associated with the choices they identify.

Chapter 2   (text page 59)

1. Students should show they realize Jerry is having trouble because he is not able to take advantage of the *division of labor, specialization,* or *specialized tools,* and that he is unable to *accumulate* much *wealth* because his business is so small and he does most things himself.

2. There are many products students could identify. One example would be movie cameras. Few people would want to buy a movie camera now because they would rather have a portable video camera. Stores must stock *what* their customers want to buy. Most video cameras sold in this country in recent years were manufactured in other countries where costs were lower. This is *how* firms thought they could make the most profit. Stores that shifted their stock to video cameras often made large profits. Their profits allowed the question *for whom* to be for them.

PART 2

UNDERSTANDING HOW INDIVIDUALS AND BUSINESSES MAKE ECONOMIC DECISIONS

CHAPTER 3

Demand and Supply (text pages 62–91)

SECTION A. The Elements of an Economic System (text pages 64–68)

Objectives (Lesson Focus)

Upon completion of this section, students will be able to:

- Explain the flow of money, products, and factors of production when provided with a copy of a circular flow model.
- Identify transactions that would occur in the product market.
- Identify transactions that would occur in the factor market.

Preparation (Instruction: Pre-teaching—Vocabulary or Activity)

1. Discussion Introduce this section by asking each student to list their sources of income and several products they frequently buy. Draw a large circular flow model on the board and place the information from the students' lists in the appropriate places on the chart. It is likely that part or all of their income is the result of their parents' earnings in the factor market rather than their own. This does not change the fact that their spending in the product market depends on earnings in the factor market. Also, wages paid in the factor market depend on sales in the product market. The parts of the model are interdependent just as parts of the real economic system depend on one another.

2. The Personal Narrative The Personal Narrative in Section A (and those in the other sections of Chapter 3) describes how a farm in the Midwest fits into the U.S. economic system in the mid-1970s. The subject of the Narrative is a young man who grew up on the farm. He discusses resources that his family purchased in the factor market and how their earnings were spent in the product market. These activities are placed into the circular flow model in the rest of this section.

The Narrative will help students see how their own spending and earnings are a part of the circular flow model.

Teaching Suggestions (Modeling/Guided Practice)

1. Give your students a copy of Discussion Topic 2 from the *Teacher's Resource Binder*. Ask them to read the news story and discuss how it relates to the circular flow model.

2. Discuss ways people receive income. Although wages are the largest part of the flow of money through the factor market, interest, rents, and profits are also parts of that flow. Point out that money which people deposit in a bank can be loaned to firms to help them produce goods and services. Depositors are paid interest by the bank for the use of their money which they can then spend in the product market. When a farmer rents land to a business, the same type of events occur.

3. Provide students with copies of a local newspaper. Ask them to cut out news articles or advertisements that concern

the transfer of money. These could include "help wanted" ads, food ads, bank ads, articles about new buildings, etc. Ask your students to explain (either orally or in writing) where each transaction would be placed on the circular flow model.

Lesson Checkpoint

Text: Self-Check, text page 66
Answers

1. A sale of crude oil would be found in the factor market.
2. A sale of a TV set would be found in the product market.
3. They are equal in value.

Follow-up Assignments   (Independent Practice/Extension/Homework)

Text: Applying What You Have Learned, text page 67
Answers

a. Selling vegetables is part of the product market.
b. Renting land from Mr. Sims is part of the factor market.
c. Hiring extra workers is part of the factor market.
d. Going to a movie is part of the product market.
e. Selling corn to a co-op is part of the product market.
f. Buying seed is part of the factor market.
g. Buying gas to drive to Cedar Rapids is part of the product market.
h. Hiring Mr. Sims is part of the factor market.
i. Buying a pair of jeans is part of the product market.

    (It is possible to put some of these transactions in other locations on

the flow model. For example, buying gas may be a part of the factor market if it is used to run tractors or to transport seed for planting.)

Section Evaluation

Self-Check, text page 66
Understanding Economics, questions 1 and 2 (Chapter 3 Review, text pages 88–90)

SECTION B.   The Law of Demand (text pages 69–72)

Objectives   (Lesson Focus)

Upon completion of this section, students will be able to:

- Restate the law of demand.
- Read a demand schedule and a demand curve.
- Draw a demand curve from a demand schedule.
- Identify and explain four determinants of demand: tastes, income, the price of related products, and number of customers.

Preparation   (Instruction: Pre-teaching— Vocabulary or Activity)

1. Discussion   Introduce this section by asking students what they would do if they inherited $1,000. How would their spending change? Would they simply buy more of what they already buy, or would they purchase different products? Point out the fact that demand is more than a desire to buy something; it is the ability and willingness to actually buy it. Changes in income, tastes, and the other determinants of demand cause people to demand either more or less of a product *if its price does not change.*

2. The Personal Narrative   The Personal Narrative in Section B continues the story of the farm in Iowa. It describes how the farm prospered due to the sale of food to the Soviet Union which increased demand for agricultural products in the 1970s. The father in the Narrative uses his increased income to buy more goods in the product market.

The Narrative demonstrates the fact that demand may change for a variety of reasons: among them, an increase in the number of customers.

Teaching Suggestions (Modeling/Guided Practice)

1. Take a survey of students in your class concerning how many of them would buy a school lunch at various prices. Use the results to complete a demand schedule similar to the one below. Either plot the data from the demand schedule as a demand curve on the board, or have students draw their own curves at their seats.

Lunch Price	Number Demanded
$1.50	_____
$1.25	_____
$1.00	_____
$ .75	_____
$ .50	_____
$ .25	_____

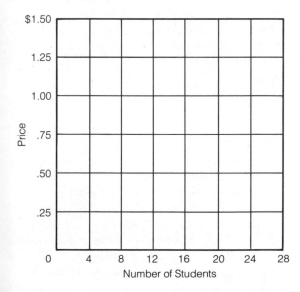

2. Assign students to think of five examples of complementary products and five examples of substitute products. Write some of their examples on the board and discuss how changes in the price of one of the paired items would cause the demand curve for the other to move.

3. Provide students with the list of firms below. Tell them that they have $5,000 to invest in one or more of the firms. They should explain (in writing or orally) why they would or would not want to invest in each type of firm. Point out how future demand is related to the number of customers a firm expects to serve.

   a. a firm that makes equipment for nursing homes

   b. a firm that makes playground equipment for new schools

   c. a firm that makes replacement parts for propellor-driven planes

   d. a firm that makes cloth baby diapers

4. If it is possible in your school, have students sell apples or large cookies outside the school cafeteria during lunch periods. On the first day charge $.50 for each item. On the second day lower the price to $.40. On the third and final day charge $.30. Keep careful records of the number of items sold each day. Your students can use this data to make a demand schedule and to draw a demand curve for their product. Be sure the student body is not aware that the price will fall each day. The expectation of falling prices could change current demand.

Lesson Checkpoint

Text: Self-Check, text page 72
        Answers

1. Wanting a new coat becomes demand when the new coat is actually sold.

2. The number of products sold should decrease.

3. Economists call these factors the determinants of demand.

Follow-up Assignments   (Independent Practice/Extension/Homework)

Text: Applying What You Have Learned, text page 72
Answer

The bad harvests in Russia from 1971 to 1973 resulted in the American sale of large quantities of grain to the Soviet Union. The number of potential customers was the determinant that resulted in a growth in demand.

Section Evaluation

Self-Check, text page 72
Understanding Economics, questions 3 and 4 (Chapter 3 Review, text pages 88–90)

SECTION C.   The Law of Supply (text pages 73–76)

Objectives   (Lesson Focus)

Upon completion of this section, students will be able to:

- Restate the law of supply.
- Read a supply schedule and a supply curve.
- Draw a supply curve from a supply schedule.
- Explain how and why changes in the costs of production change supply.

Preparation   (Instruction: Pre-teaching— Vocabulary or Activity)

1. Discussion   Introduce this section by giving each student a 3-by-5 card. Tell them to describe on the card the job they are expected to do at home that they like *least*. Washing dishes could be an example. On the back of the card, have them write how much they would be willing to pay someone else to do the job for them (if they had an income of $50 a week).

Collect the cards. Read several jobs to the class telling how much the person would be willing to pay. Ask how many students would do the job for the suggested amount and write the number on the board. Increase the amount of pay several times and ask the students each time how many would do the work. By recording their answers, you will create a supply schedule for the service. Use the supply schedule to draw a supply curve.

2. The Personal Narrative   The Personal Narrative for Section C continues the story of the farm in Iowa. It describes the growth in supply of agricultural products that occurred in response to increased demand in the 1970s. The subject's father used his increased income and borrowed money to purchase additional resources in the factor market. Other farmers did the same. As a result, the production of farm products surpassed their demand by the early 1980s.

The Narrative demonstrates that a firm's willingness to supply products changes with its costs of production and expectations of being able to sell additional products.

Teaching Suggestions   (Modeling/Guided Practice)

1. Invite an admissions counselor from a local college or vocational school to speak to your class about their institution. After their presentation, discuss the value of the service they were selling with your class. How is supplying an education different from supplying food, furniture, or clothing? How much more does it cost the school to educate another student? Why do private training schools tend to

start up in areas with high rates of unemployment? What product are they supplying? How are they responding to a change in demand?

2. Describe the following situation to your class:

> There is a community in the western part of the United States, near a wilderness area that has a river in a deep valley. The area is used by campers, hunters, and by many other people.
>
> There is a high rate of unemployment in the community. A local business has offered to expand its factory and add 500 jobs if it can be supplied with inexpensive electric power. A dam and hydroelectric project in the wilderness area could provide the power. The project would flood most of the river valley. The state has to decide whether to allow an electric company to build the dam so the factory can grow.

> Ask your students to consider the problem. If the dam is built, what would happen to the firm's willingness to supply products to the market? What would the costs and benefits of the decision be? Do your students feel the dam should be built?

3. Use Discussion Topic 3 from the *Teacher's Resource Binder* to illustrate the use of a supply curve and the effects of changes in the costs of production.

Lesson Checkpoint

Text: Self-Check, text page 76
     Answers

1. The number of products for sale will increase.
2. The cost of additional units of production will increase.
3. The number of products offered for sale will decrease.

Follow-up Assignments   (Independent Practice/Extension/Homework)

Text: Applying What You Have Learned, text page 76
     Answer

The farmers decided to make the investments necessary to increase production because the price of corn had gone up.

Section Evaluation

Self-Check, text page 76
Understanding Economics, questions 5 and 6 (Chapter 3 Review, text pages 88–90)

SECTION D.   Surpluses, Shortages, and Equilibrium (text pages 77–80)

Objectives   (Lesson Focus)

Upon completion of this section, students will be able to:

- Identify and explain the meaning of equilibrium.
- Explain how surpluses or shortages tend to force prices to the equilibrium price in a market economy.

Preparation   (Instruction: Pre-teaching—Vocabulary or Activity)

1. Discussion   Introduce this section by giving students a list of products and asking them to find the current price for each item in advertising supplements from a local newspaper. Items could include specific brands of soap, foods, or personal care items. Your students should find that most stores charge about the same price for similar items (although many stores will have loss–leaders to attract shoppers). Discuss how the forces of demand and supply interact to reach a market price. What would an individual store find if it charged substantially more or less than other stores for the same item?

2. The Personal Narrative The Personal Narrative in Section D continues the story of the farm in Iowa. It describes how the excess supply of agricultural products forced prices down and eventually led to bankruptcy for many farmers. It emphasizes the problem farmers had in repaying loans taken out when prices were high with reduced income earned when prices were low.

The Narrative will help students understand how the forces of demand and supply interact to set prices. It shows that the price a firm can sell its product for may have little to do with the amount the firm paid to make the product.

Teaching Suggestions (Modeling/Guided Practice)

1. Use the Demand and Supply Cards in the *Teacher's Resource Binder*. Hand out copies of the cards to your students. Give about two-thirds of them "Demand Cards" and the rest "Supply Cards." The difference between the cards reflect different tastes and levels of income for consumers, or costs of production for producers.

   Read off the different possible prices in class and ask each person how many products he/she would demand or supply according to his/her card. Tabulate these quantities on the board and make them into a demand and supply schedule. Convert the schedules into a graph of demand and supply. What is the equilibrium price and quantity that has been identified on the graph?

2. Your students may enjoy producing an imitation of the television show, "The Price is Right." Choose a panel of four students who will guess the true market price of various items. Those who are closest to the correct price without going over will win the item. Using humorous

items, such as fish food or purple hair spray, can help to hold student attention. When they are finished, discuss the idea of equilibrium price as it applies to the items used as prizes.

3. Point out the fact that there are always end-of-season sales in which stores attempt to sell leftover items like summer clothes or snow shovels. Ask your students to explain what is happening to the location of demand curves that causes stores to reduce their prices. Why do changing seasons change the location of the point of equilibrium? What would happen to the store's sales and inventories if it refused to lower its prices as customer demand fell?

Lesson Checkpoint

Text: Self-Check, text page 80
Answers

1. The point of equilibrium is found at the intersection of the supply and demand curves.

2. It must lower its price to eliminate its surplus.

3. If the firm is charging less than the equilibrium price, it will have a surplus of product. This will encourage it to increase its price.

Follow-up Assignments (Independent Practice/Extension/Homework)

Text: Applying What You Have Learned, text page 80
Answer

The price of corn in any year is the result of the interaction of demand and supply. An overall shortage of supply causes an increase in price, and so a farm might make a profit even though crops are poor. An overall surplus of corn causes the market price to fall, and so a farm might make no profit even though crops are good. However, crop failure on a single farm, when all other farms are having a good year, will not produce a shortage in the market, and so will not cause a price increase.

Section Evaluation

Self-Check, text page 80

SECTION E.   Elasticity (text pages 81–86)

Objectives   (Lesson Focus)

Upon completion of this section, students will be able to:

- Identify demand as being price elastic or price inelastic when given appropriate examples.
- Recognize the relationship between percentage changes in price and resulting percentage changes in the quantity sold that demonstrate a product's price elasticity of demand.
- Identify characteristics of products that tend to make their demand either price elastic or price inelastic.
- Identify situations in which a product's price elasticity of demand has economic importance.

Preparation   (Instruction: Pre-teaching—Vocabulary or Activity)

1. Discussion   Introduce this section by asking students how much they would pay to hear music played by a local group that is not very popular or talented. They would probably be willing to pay a dollar or two, but no more. If the group charged $5.00 for tickets, they would sell few. Explain that the demand for their music is quite elastic. As the price

increases, the quantity demanded falls rapidly.

Then ask your students how much they would pay to see a famous national rock star (you supply the name). It is likely that your class, as a group, would buy about the same number of tickets at $5, $10, $15, or even $20. Explain that the demand for music played by famous performers is quite inelastic. A change in price results in relatively little change in the quantity demanded.

2. The Personal Narrative   The Personal Narrative in Section E continues the story of the farm in Iowa. It demonstrates the fact that demand for some products is more sensitive to changes in price than demand for other products. The subject of the Narrative comes to realize that people need about the same amount of food each year. If production grows beyond what people need, the product cannot be easily sold and prices will fall rapidly. On the other hand, shortages of food cause prices to increase just as rapidly.

The Narrative will help students understand the difference between elastic demand and inelastic demand. It also shows how price elasticity of demand can affect individual firms.

Teaching Suggestions   (Modeling/Guided Practice)

1. Give students Discussion Topic 4 from the *Teacher's Resource Binder,* describing a hypothetical situation about an essential medicine that is too expensive for many people to afford. Help your class identify the issues involved in this question. Divide your class into teams to debate whether or not the government should provide the drug.

2. Ask your students to list five products they believe are necessities and five they believe are luxuries. Have them find the

current market price for these products. Tell them to assume that the price for all of the products just went up by 50 percent. Assign them to write a paper in which they predict the percentage decline in sales that would result from the increase in price for each product. If they believe the sales would be cut by more than half, the demand is elastic. If they believe the sales would be cut by less than half, the demand in inelastic. Your students should find that the demand for necessities is less elastic than the demand for luxuries.

3. Explain that when firms advertise, they are often trying to change the price elasticity of demand for their products. If they can convince their customers that their product is necessary and that no similar product is as good as theirs, they will be able to charge more for their product while losing few customers. They are trying to make the demand for their product more price inelastic. Have students bring in or identify advertisements that are intended to do this.

Lesson Checkpoint

Text: Self-Check, text page 86
      Answers

1. Elasticity describes this relationship.
2. The demand is price elastic.
3. The demand is price inelastic.

Follow-up Assignments   (Independent Practice/Extension/Homework)

1. Text: Applying What You Have Learned, text page 86
      Answers

    a. Demand for one brand of

toothpaste is elastic because there are many other brands that can be substituted.

    b. Demand for trips to Florida in July is elastic because it is warm in most places and there are also other places to go.

    c. Demand for heart disease medicine is inelastic because it is very important to its consumers.

    d. Demand for tickets to a reading of English poetry probably is very elastic because the students would probably rather not attend.

    e. Demand for tickets to a rock concert may be quite inelastic if many people want to attend.

    f. Demand for water by people lost in the desert would be very inelastic since its use would keep them alive.

2. Teacher's Resource Binder: Critical Thinking Activity for Chapter 3 (answers in Binder).

Section Evaluation

Self-Check, text page 86
Understanding Economics, question 7 (Chapter 3 Review, text pages 88–90)

ADDITIONAL MATERIALS FOR CHAPTER 3

Chapter Evaluation

Teacher's Resource Binder: Chapter 3 Quiz

Reteaching and Extension

See the *Teacher's Resource Binder* and the *Student Activity Guide* for additional handouts and activities for Chapter 3.

TEACHER'S BIBLIOGRAPHY FOR CHAPTER 3

Economics Sources

Clawson, Elmer U. *Our Economy: How it Works*, 2nd ed. Reading, Mass. Addison-Wesley, 1984. See Chapter 2, "From Canvas to Cut-offs: The Jeans Story," for a good description of demand, supply, and pricing.

McConnell, Campbell R. *Economics: Principles, Problems, and Policies*, 10th ed. New York: McGraw-Hill Book Co., 1987. Chapter 4 on the mechanics of demand, supply, and pricing and Chapter 5 for examples and an evaluation of the pricing system are well done. See Chapter 24 for elasticity.

Miller, Roger LeRoy. *Economics Today*, 5th ed. New York: Harper and Row, 1985. See Chapters 2 and 3 for demand and supply and Chapter 19 for elasticity of demand.

References for Additional Teaching Strategies

Morton, John, et al. *High School Economics Courses*. New York: Joint Council on Economic Education, 1985. For lesson plans and student handouts, see Lessons 5, 6, 7, and 10.

Harwich, George. *The Economics of Energy: A Teaching Kit* (Grades 7–12). New York: Joint Council on Economic Education, 1983. Lessons and materials for teaching the demand, supply, and pricing of energy.

CHAPTER 3 REVIEW ANSWERS

Building Your Vocabulary   (text page 89)

1. supply
2. demand
3. product market
4. factor market
5. price inelastic demand
6. price elastic demand
7. demand schedule
8. supply curve
9. diminishing returns
10. circular flow model
11. supply schedule
12. demand curve
13. complementary goods
14. substitutes
15. surplus
16. law of demand
17. shortage
18. elasticity
19. point of equilibrium
20. determinants of demand
21. law of supply

Understanding Economics   (text page 90)

1. Three of the many possible transactions that could take place in the product market include:

   a. the purchase of a meal at a restaurant
   b. the purchase of a bus ticket
   c. the purchase of a pair of socks

   All purchases in the product market involve consumer goods and services that are used to directly satisfy human wants.

2. Three of the many transactions that could take place in the factor market include:

   a. paying someone to cut your lawn
   b. buying supplies for your restaurant
   c. paying for land to build a factory on

   All purchases in the factor market involve goods or services that will be used to produce something else that will eventually satisfy human wants.

3. If you want or need something, it will do a firm and the economy little good if you cannot also buy it. There is no profit to be made from a product people want but don't buy.

4. a. A blizzard would increase the demand for snow tires by changing tastes and preferences.

   b. The demand for tea would decrease when the price of coffee falls, because tea and coffee are substitutes.

   c. The demand for specialty food decreases in a recession because people have lower incomes and do not buy as many luxury items.

   d. The demand for housing increases when people move to avoid crime because of a change in tastes and preferences.

5. Diminishing productivity occurs when, as more factors of production are added to the production of a product, the resulting increase in production keeps getting smaller. This happens because (a) there is a limit to how many workers can be used efficiently in a factory, and (b) there is also a limit to the number of machines that can be placed in a factory without causing overcrowding.

6. a. The supply would increase if the cost of a product's basic raw material went down.

   b. The supply would decrease if the wages paid to workers increased.

   c. The supply would increase if a new machine reduced waste.

   d. The supply would increase if a firm converted to gas from electricity. The only reason to convert would be to reduce costs of production.

7. a. If the demand for a product is price elastic, a change in price will cause a greater percent change in the number sold.

   b. One would expect the price elasticity for medicine to be inelastic if there were few substitutes for such important products.

   c. If a firm raises the price of its brand of dish soap by 10 percent, one would expect a larger than 10 percent drop in sales because there are many other brands of soap consumers could buy.

Thinking Critically About Economics (text page 90)

1. Virtually any job could be used. The students should make it clear that they understand that labor supplied to a firm in the factor market allows people to buy goods and services in the product market.

2. Any changes that would affect the determinants of demand would be acceptable. Be sure not to accept a change in price that _would not_ change demand. Three possible answers are:

   a. Advertise to convince people your shoes are wonderful.

   b. Move your store to a town where people have higher incomes.

   c. Stock a larger supply of different types of shoes.

3. If the items listed are important, the probability is that many of them will have price inelastic demand. Many of these will end up being a "judgment call." For example, the demand for a hamburger is elastic for most people, but some people may really prefer one particular product. Be sure to note that although an individual may have product loyalty, this would not be true of large groups.

Special Skills Projects   (text page 90)

1. Be sure that the poster is set up the same way as in the text.
2. You will probably find that there is a wide variation in the number of television sets each family owns. Family size is frequently a determining factor. Income does not always have much to do with it. You might discuss why this is often the case. Perhaps such people cannot afford other types of entertainment.

CHAPTER 4

The Consumer and the Economy: Getting What You Pay For (text pages 92–113)

SECTION A.   How We Make Spending Decisions (text pages 94–97)

Objectives   (Lesson Focus)

Upon completion of this section, students will be able to:

- Define the principle of diminishing marginal utility and recognize situations that demonstrate this principle.
- Explain how the slope of a demand curve demonstrates the principle of diminishing marginal utility.

Preparation   (Instruction: Pre-teaching— Vocabulary or Activity)

1. Discussion   Introduce this section by assigning students to identify the one item they feel they most need now, and to explain why they need it. Ask your students to describe how much they would want a second unit of the item if they were given the first unit. Ask them why a second unit might not be as important to them as the first was. Would they want something else instead?

Explain how the fact that most students would not find a second unit to be worth as much as the first demonstrates the principle of diminishing marginal utility.

It is possible to complete this exercise by giving students a fictional amount of money to spend. They will probably choose to distribute their spending among many items.

2. The Personal Narrative   The Personal Narrative for Section A describes a person who wants to own sports cars to the point of obsession. The subject of the Narrative gives up as many other goods and services as possible to save for a car. The point is made that normal people do not behave this way. They distribute their spending among many items to maximize the utility they obtain from their income.

The Narrative describes a situation that will help students understand the principle of diminishing marginal utility and how it affects the way they spend their money.

Teaching Suggestions   (Modeling/Guided Practice)

1. Ask your students to count the number of television sets they have in their homes and put the number on a piece of paper. Collect the papers and tabulate the results on the chalkboard. Discuss why some families have many more sets than others. What might explain the difference? Could it show a difference in individual values? Point out that diminishing marginal utility does not mean everyone has the same values. One person might feel one television was enough while another might want three or four.
2. Many stores offer discounts for large quantity purchases. However, many customers choose to buy small quantities that cost more per amount. An example might be ice cream that costs $3.59 per

half gallon or $1.19 per pint. The half gallon is four times as large as a pint, but only costs three times as much. Still, many people buy pints of ice cream. Ask students to explain what this has to do with the principle of diminishing marginal utility.

3. Ask your students to predict the ending to the following story which demonstrates diminishing marginal utility:

Johnny entered a contest in his newspaper and won. He was thrilled because the prize was being able to ride a rollercoaster as often as he wanted to at a local amusement park. He got to the park at 9:00 AM so that he would be able to ride it as many times as possible. At the start of the day he felt very happy. By 10:00 AM, he . . .

Lesson Checkpoint

Text: Self-Check, text page 97
Answers

1. The second television set would be of less value.
2. After a person has a few of them, additional ones become less important.

Follow-up Assignments (Independent Practice/Extension/Homework)

Text: Applying What You Have Learned, text page 97
Answers

Student answers will vary. It is probable that some of your students will find that some of the items they buy in small quantity are the most important to them. For example, students would not buy more than one calculator, but having one is very important if they are taking math. This would demon-

strate the principle of diminishing marginal utility. The first one would be very important, but there would be little point (utility) in having more than one.

Section Evaluation

Self-Check, text page 97
Thinking Critically About Economics, question 1 (Chapter 4 Review, text pages 109–111)

SECTION B. Consumer Sovereignty (text pages 98–101)

Objectives (Lesson Focus)

Upon completion of this section, students will be able to:

- Explain the meaning of the term, "consumer sovereignty," and its relationship to the way the basic economic question, *what*, is answered in capitalism.

- Explain the meaning of the term *invisible hand* and its relationship to maintaining competition in price and quality in capitalism.

Preparation (Instruction: Pre-teaching—Vocabulary or Activity)

1. Discussion Introduce this section by giving students a copy of a clothing advertisement taken from a newspaper that is five to ten years old (most libraries can help you make a copy of such an advertisement). Be sure to choose one that shows clothing that is currently out of style. Ask your students to write a brief essay in which they describe what would happen to a store that tried to sell these clothes now. Have several students read their essays in class and discuss what they had to say. In general, students will recognize the problem a store would have in selling dated styles. The discussion can then be led into the topics of consumer sovereignty and the invisible hand.

2. The Personal Narrative The Personal Narrative in Section B describes a situation that demonstrates the idea of consumer sovereignty and the invisible hand. The subject of the Narrative is a young woman who owns a boutique that specializes in selling fashionable clothing at reduced prices. To succeed in her business, she is forced to offer products that her customers want to buy. She earns her profit by working very hard to provide products her customers want at low prices. By looking out for her own interests, she also serves those of her customers.

The Narrative will help students appreciate the limited freedom businesses have in a competitive market economy. In many ways they are forced to make decisions by their customers and by competition.

Teaching Suggestions (Modeling/Guided Practice)

1. In most areas there are one or two radio stations that young people listen to more than others. There are other stations that appeal to older people. The types of advertising heard on these stations is likely to be very different. The radio stations are in business to sell air-time to advertisers. Discuss factors that make a radio station successful with your class. How does the fact that it is hard to find stations that play "classical" music in many areas relate to consumer sovereignty?

2. Hand out copies of Discussion Topic 5 from the *Teacher's Resource Binder*. Discuss how the story is related to the ideas of consumer sovereignty and the invisible hand.

3. If there is a local farmer's market, assign several students to survey the prices charged by different farmers for the same types of produce. They should find that all the farmers charge almost the exact same price for produce of equal quality. Ask your students to explain why the farmers do this, and how it demonstrates the idea of the invisible hand.

Lesson Checkpoint

Text: Self-Check, text page 101
       Answers

1. To sell products, producers must meet consumer needs. This is consumer sovereignty.

2. The "invisible hand" means that producers will serve the interests of society when they attempt to serve their own interests.

Follow-up Assignments   (Independent Practice/Extension/Homework)

Text: Applying What You Have Learned, text page 101
       Answers

The determination of how many pink polka dot dresses and baggy pants will be manufactured in the next year will be based on the items' previous desirability by consumers. If these items sold well and are still considered popular by the consumer, they will likely be a manufacturing priority again. If not, manufacturers will likely limit or discontinue the items altogether.

Section Evaluation

Self-Check, text page 101
Understanding Economics, questions 1 and 2 (Chapter 4 Review, text pages 109–111)

SECTION C.   Individual Freedom and Consumer Protection (text pages 102–105)

Objectives   (Lesson Focus)

Upon completion of this section, students will be able to:

- Describe why there has been a growing need for government consumer protection as the economy has grown over the past 200 years.
- Identify and explain several of the trade-offs that are made when the government undertakes consumer protection.

Preparation   (Instruction: Pre-teaching— Vocabulary or Activity)

1. Discussion   Introduce this section by asking students to make a list of at least five ways in which they are affected by government regulations intended to protect them. The warning on cigarettes, seatbelt laws, drinking ages, being required to attend school, and speed limits are some examples. Ask them to explain the reasoning behind each rule and to give their opinion of the need for the rule. Do they feel that their parents would have the same opinions they have? Why or why not?

2. The Personal Narrative   The Personal Narrative for Section C tells the story of a man who wants the government to stay out of his life, at least most of the time. The subject of the Narrative is a young person whose uncle is offended by the government's regulations which are intended to protect consumers. He resents warnings on cigarette packages and seatbelt laws. However, he expects the government to help him when he feels he has been cheated.

The Narrative demonstrates the trade-off between the costs and benefits of government consumer protection.

Teaching Suggestions   (Modeling/Guided Practice)

1. Many states have passed "lemon laws" that make an auto dealer responsible for making repairs to used cars they sell. Dealers have argued that such laws force them to charge much more for used cars. They say the law causes many people to buy used cars that are defective from private individuals who are not covered by the law. They suggest that poor people will be hurt by the law because they won't be able to afford decent transportation. Other people argue that poor people will benefit because they won't be sold "junk" cars by dishonest dealers.

   Organize a debate in your class based on this topic. Do students believe the law is a good or bad idea? Is it a reasonable type of consumer protection? Should these laws be extended to other products?

2. Use Discussion Topic 6 from the *Teacher's Resource Binder* to discuss an issue relating to consumer protection, government regulation, and First Amendment rights.

3. Have your students cut out "ingredients labels" from foods they eat and bring them to class. Discuss whether or not the labels provide useful information, and whether people really pay attention to them. Should the government require more specific information on all labels, such as amounts of each ingredient, or breakdowns on fats, proteins, and carbohydrates?

Lesson Checkpoint

Text: Self-Check, text page 105
Answers

1. Products are much more complicated today.

2. Additional money must be spent

to meet regulations, and this cost is passed on to the consumers.

3. Trade-offs include reduced competition and a slower acceptance of new ideas.

Follow-up Assignments   (Independent Practice/Extension/Homework)

Text: Applying What You Have Learned, text page 105
   Answers

1. The answers in this exercise will depend on the students' individual values. Their explanations should be clear. Class discussions of these points can lead to important understandings of why people have different opinions and values.

2. Included in the picture are the following government-regulated activities:

   a. traffic signals and regulations

   b. taxi service

   c. telephone service

   d. billboards (size restrictions in some cities)

   e. lighting (government-regulated utility)

Section Evaluation

Self-Check, text page 205
Understanding Economics, questions 3 and 4 (Chapter 4 Review, text pages 109–111)

SECTION D.   Advertising and Consumer Demand (text pages 106–108)

Objective   (Lesson Focus)

Upon completion of this section, students will be able to:

■ Identify and explain the difference be-

tween advertising that is intended to inform and advertising that is intended to persuade.

Preparation   (Instruction: Pre-teaching—Vocabulary or Activity)

1. Discussion   Introduce this section by asking students to make a list of specific advertisements they find obnoxious or of little value, and a second list they feel are valuable to them. These lists may be done either by individual students or in groups. Ask the students to explain what there is about each ad that makes it good or bad from the point of view of the consumer. Why do some firms use advertisements that are clearly obnoxious?

2. The Personal Narrative   The Personal Narrative for Section D concerns a young woman and how she is affected by advertising. Although the subject of the Narrative professes to see no value in advertising, she repeatedly is influenced by it. She uses advertising to remind herself of things she needs to do, as a source on information so she can make better decisions, and ultimately as a source of personal income.

The Narrative shows students how advertising affects people like themselves. It demonstrates the difference between advertising that is intended to persuade and that which is intended to inform.

Teaching Suggestions   (Modeling/Guided Practice)

1. Many states have outlawed advertising on major interstate highways to make them more attractive. They feel travelers would rather look at the scenery than at a collection of billboards. The owners of businesses often say this reduces their sales and does not serve the interests of travelers. When someone is looking for a

place to stay or eat, they don't know where to stop. They may have to keep getting off the road to ask or they may miss good places. Ask your students to discuss this issue and see if they can reach a consensus on what limits should be placed on highway advertising.

2. Choose several products your students are likely to purchase and assign each student to write two newspaper ads for one of the products. Their first advertisement should be informative. The second should be intended to persuade. Have them read their ads in class and discuss the factors that make them likely to succeed. Remember the purpose of the advertisement is to alter consumer demand, not just to entertain.

3. Assign students to interview local businesspeople about their use of advertising. Students should ask questions about how the firm decides what sort of advertising to use, where and when to advertise, how much to spend on advertising, and how they measure the success of their advertising. Students should report their findings to the class. Help your students find common factors among the various firms.

Lesson Checkpoint

Text: Self-Check, text page 108
 Answers

1. Firms advertise to increase demand for their products.

2. Informative advertising gives actual differences between products. Persuasive advertising attempts to change the customer's tastes or preferences.

3. One reason that persuasive advertising is sometimes considered harmful to consumers is that such

advertising can convince people—especially children—to buy products that are not healthy for them.

Follow-up Assignments   (Independent Practice/Extension/Homework)

1. Text: Applying What You Have Learned, text page 108
 Answers

   a. Sherry looked at want ads in the paper.   *inform*

   b. Sherry found out about a shoe sale.   *inform*

   c. Sherry was reminded of Mother's Day.   *inform*

   d. Sherry found out about a new play.   *persuade*

   e. Sherry heard of an inexpensive diet program.   *inform*

2. Teachers Resource Binder: Critical Thinking Activity, Chapter 4 (answers in Binder)

Section Evaluation

Self-Check, text page 108
Understanding Economics, questions 5 and 6 (Chapter 4 Review, text pages 109–111)

ADDITIONAL MATERIALS FOR CHAPTER 4

Chapter Evaluation

Teacher's Resource Binder: Chapter 4 Quiz

Reteaching and Extension

See the *Teacher's Resource Binder* and the *Student Activity Guide* for additional handouts and activities for Chapter 4.

TEACHER'S BIBLIOGRAPHY FOR CHAPTER 4

Economics Sources

Carson, Robert B. *Economic Issues Today: Alternative Approaches*. New York: St. Martin's Press, 1987. See "Consumer Protection: the Matter of Automobile Safety."

Gordon, Sanford D. and Dawson, George G. *Introductory Economics*, 6th ed. Lexington, Mass.: D. C. Heath, Inc., 1987. Chapter 10 provides a good overview of the weaknesses in consumer sovereignty, consumer protection and the pro and con of advertising.

McConnell, Campbell R. *Economics: Principles, Problems, and Policies*, 10th ed. New York: McGraw-Hill Book Co., 1987. See Chapter 25 for the theory of consumer behavior.

References for Additional Teaching Strategies

Niss, James R., et al. *Basic Business and Consumer Education*. New York: Joint Council on Economic Education, 1979. Lesson plans, handouts, and a glossary suitable for dealing with basic business or consumer education.

Ristau, Robert, et al. *Basic Business and Consumer Education*. New York: Joint Council on Economic Education, 1985. Detailed lesson plans, handouts, and sources for other information on most aspects of consumer economics.

CHAPTER 4 REVIEW ANSWERS

Building Your Vocabulary   (text page 110)

1. persuasive advertising
2. consumer protection
3. consumer sovereignty
4. informative advertising
5. invisible hand
6. diminishing marginal utility

Understanding Economics   (text page 111)

1. A firm that sells wooden wagon wheels will have difficulty staying in business because there is very little demand for this product.

2. To earn a profit, producers in competition must sell products of similar quality and price or their customers will buy elsewhere. If Joe is charging an excessive price for inferior tires, few people would buy from him. It is as if there were an "invisible hand" forcing him to do what his competition does.

3. Most people believe the government should regulate the production and distribution of chemicals and similar products because few consumers have the knowledge to make these decisions for themselves.

4. The trade-off is between environmental safety and additional production. The chemical could increase crop yields but would make people sick at the same time.

5. The advertisements used by the students should include specific information that would help consumers make rational choices in how they spend their money.

6. The advertisements used by the students should be misleading and intended to convince consumers to do something that could be harmful to them.

Thinking Critically About Economics   (text page 111)

1. The price a consumer is willing to pay for a product is a measure of the value or utility that it would provide to the con-

sumer. If John would pay $50 for his first jacket but only $20 for a second one, the second one is of less value to him. This demonstrates the principle of diminishing marginal utility.

2. Today few people would buy sack dresses. A store that tried to sell them would do poorly. This demonstrates the idea of consumer sovereignty: Firms must sell what consumers are willing to buy.

3. If a firm offers inferior products at higher prices than other firms charge in competition, they will sell few products, make little profit, and probably go out of business. This is the idea behind the invisible hand.

4. Providing information about the nutritive value of all food offered in a restaurant would be very costly. Servings would have to be measured for uniformity and nutritive values. This would have to be done by specialists and would cost a great deal of money. It would also prevent the business from offering new dishes. The price of the food would be forced up and the number of choices on the menu would be reduced.

5. The students' advertisements should be clearly informative and persuasive. Real ads are often mixed, but in this artificial situation you can require them to be all one or the other.

Special Skills Projects   (text page 111)

1. You will probably find that most of your students feel the ban is justified. This may be the result of having grown up with various forms of public smoking restrictions. If the same survey were taken among their parents, there might be a different result. You would likely find stronger reactions to outlawing public smoking.

2. Your students will find that the prices are much the same in similar stores if no sale is being offered. Stores of different size and location will have different prices because they are offering something other than just the product. They may be closer to home, or open longer hours.

CHAPTER 5

Business and the Economy (text pages 114–139)

SECTION A.   Forms of Business Organization (text pages 116–121)

Objectives   (Lesson Focus)

Upon completion of this section, students will be able to:

- Identify and describe the basic characteristics of single proprietorships, partnerships, and corporations.
- Identify and explain the advantages of corporations which have allowed them to dominate production in the U.S. economy.

Preparation   (Instruction: Pre-teaching—Vocabulary or Activity)

1. Discussion   Introduce this section by reviewing the factors of production. Ask students how these factors can be brought together to create goods and services. Point out that owners must have money to finance new businesses. The form of business organization chosen depends at least in part on the amount of money that is needed.

A second important point is that all businesses involve an element of risk. New businesses usually have more risk than older, more established firms. People may be hesitant to invest in a firm unless there is a way to limit their exposure to risk.

A final consideration is the degree to which individuals want to be involved in the management of a firm. This may determine the type of organization they choose to invest in. Many people would like to benefit from the success of a business but have little interest or skill in running a firm. Others want to help make decisions and manage the firm. These people would probably choose to invest in different types of business organizations. Having discussed these points, identify and explain the advantages and disadvantages of the three basic forms of business organization which appear on Table 5–1 in the text.

2. The Personal Narrative   The Personal Narrative for Section A (and for the following Narratives in this chapter as well) concern Rita and Joshua, a married couple, who open a restaurant. This Narrative demonstrates how they identify and solve the problems of organizing a new business. At first, they decide a partnership with Rita's father offers the best trade–off between costs and benefits for the type of business they want to run. Eventually they form a corporation to allow their business to grow.

The Narrative demonstrates the types of decisions that must be made when a new business is organized.

Teaching Suggestions   (Modeling/Guided Practice)

1. Identify several types of businesses that can be found in your community. Ask students, either as individuals or in groups, to choose the type of business organization that is more appropriate for each firm and to explain why.
2. Use Discussion Topic 7 from the *Teacher's Resource Binder* which asks students how they would organize a business to market

a wonderful food combination they've discovered.

Lesson Checkpoint

Text: Self-Check, text page 120
Answers

1. Unlimited liability: the owners' personal property can be taken to satisfy debts of the business. Limited liability: the individual owners cannot lose more than they have invested in the firm.
2. Partnerships can raise more money to establish the business; they can share certain kinds of expensive capital and services.
3. Corporations can raise money through the sale of stocks and bonds, have limited liability, and have unlimited life.

Follow-up Assignments   (Independent Practice/Extension/Homework)

Text: Applying What You Have Learned, text page 121

One possible ending: Joshua and Rita began to look for additional locations, but the shareholders did not agree with them on their choices. Eventually a compromise was reached, settling on locations that Joshua and Rita did not really want. Two of the new locations failed, and profits for the entire company were very low.

Joshua and Rita could keep control of the corporation by retaining at least 51 percent of the shares, but this would bring in less money from the investors. Joshua and Rita would have to either supply more of the money themselves—increasing their risk if the venture should fail—or else restrict their expansion.

Section Evaluation

Self-Check, text page 120
Understanding Economics, question 1
  (Chapter 5 Review, text pages 135–137)

SECTION B.   The Costs of Production (text pages 122–124)

Objective   (Lesson Focus)

Upon completion of this section, students will be able to:

- Identify, define, give examples of, and explain the difference between fixed and variable costs.

Preparation   (Introduction: Pre-teaching— Vocabulary or Activity)

1. Discussion   Introduce this section by giving each student a red card and a green card. Tell them that you are going to read a list of different costs of production for a firm that manufactures tennis shoes. If the cost will not change when more shoes are produced (fixed costs), they should hold up the red card. If the costs will change when more shoes are produced (variable costs), they should hold up the green card. You may want to count to three and have them all do it at once to avoid having students just copy one another. This exercise will encourage participation by all students. Explain the differences between the costs as you go along.

Costs of Production for a
Tennis Shoe Manufacturer

wages for production line workers	(variable)
salary of the firm's president	(fixed)
rubber for the soles	(variable)
cost of electricity to run machines	(variable)
property taxes on the factory	(fixed)
canvas for tops	(variable)
television advertising	(fixed)
mortgage payment on the factory	(fixed)
shipping for finished shoes	(variable)
wages for security guard	(fixed)

2. The Personal Narrative   The Personal Narrative for Section B continues the story of Rita and Joshua. The specific costs of production are identified in the Narrative. The fact that Rita and Joshua still have personal expenses to pay while they are starting their business is made.

The Narrative demonstrates the difference between fixed and variable costs.

Teaching Suggestions   (Modeling/Guided Practice)

1. Use Discussion Topic 8 from the *Teacher's Resource Binder* to discuss the significance of fixed costs when sales decline.

2. Ask your students to identify the fixed and variable costs of running their households.

3. Most students either own, or would like to own, an automobile. Help your class list the costs of having a car and to identify each cost as a fixed or variable cost.

Lesson Checkpoint

Text: Self-Check, text page 124
     Answers

1. Fixed costs must be paid regardless of how many products the firm manufactures. Variable costs change with the number of products made.

2. Fixed costs are most often underestimated.

3. Increasing the number of products sold is one way to reduce fixed costs per tire.

Follow-up Assignments   (Independent Practice/Extension/Homework)

Text: Applying What You Have Learned, text page 124
     Answers

1. Kitchen equipment—once purchased would be a fixed cost

2. Dishes & utensils—once purchased would be a fixed cost

3. Rent for six months—would be a fixed cost

4. Insurance—would be a fixed cost

5. Paper products—would be a variable cost

6. Utilities—would be a variable cost (except for minimum monthly payment)

7. Furniture—would be a fixed cost

8. Wiring and plumbing—would be a fixed cost

9. License & fees—would be a fixed cost

10. Food and inventory—would be a variable cost

11. Cash register—would be a fixed cost

12. Advertising—once contracted would be a fixed cost

Section Evaluation

Self-Check, text page 124
Understanding Economics, question 2
   (Chapter 5 Review, text pages 135–137)

SECTION C.   Reducing Average Fixed Costs (text pages 125–128)

Objective   (Lesson Focus)

Upon completion of this section, students will be able to:

- Define average fixed costs and explain the advantages that are often the result of diversification.

Preparation   (Instruction: Pre-teaching—Vocabulary or Activity)

1. Discussion   Introduce this section by

asking students how they would react to school being open year round (if your district does this already, you could ask students how it has worked out). In some districts, schools run the entire year. Students are assigned to attend school in two of three yearly semesters. Some students have winters off, while others have most of the Fall or Spring.

Explain why this has been done. It reduces the district's fixed costs per student. Fifty percent more students can be educated in the same buildings when they are run all year. Businesses do the same when they run a night shift. Can your students think of any other advantages or disadvantages of the idea?

2. The Personal Narrative   The Personal Narrative in Section C continues the story of Rita and Joshua. In this section they attempt to reduce average fixed costs by offering different items for sale. They also choose to stay open for longer hours. In this way they are able to distribute their fixed costs among more items and reduce the amount of fixed cost per item.

The Narrative demonstrates why many businesses have chosen to diversify into different markets.

Teaching Suggestions   (Modeling/Guided Practice)

1. In Section B of this chapter, students were asked to identify the fixed and variable costs of running a household. A variation on this idea is to ask them to explain how much more it costs to have a large family than a small one. Which costs do not increase with the size of the family? How can a family reduce its average fixed cost per member?

2. Use Discussion Topic 9 from the *Teacher's Resource Binder* to show the significance of reducing average fixed costs.

3. Assign your students to survey local gro-

cery stores to find non-food–related products for sale. Combine the lists on the board in class. Discuss why grocery stores stock so many non–food items.

Lesson Checkpoint

Text: Self-Check, text page 128
Answers

1. Firms can make a larger profit if they reduce average fixed costs.
2. The average fixed cost would be two dollars.
3. Selling different types of merchandise is one way of reducing average fixed costs.

Follow-Up Assignments (Independent Practice/Extension/Homework)

Text: Applying What You Have Learned, text page 128
Answers

Rita and Joshua did a number of things to reduce their average fixed costs. These include:

- expanding their menu to sell more products
- selling snack foods to children on their way home from school
- staying open for longer hours so they could sell more items

Section Evaluation

Self-Check, text page 128
Understanding Economics, question 3
(Chapter 5 Review, text pages 135–137)

SECTION D. Rent, Interest, and How Businesses Obtain Money (text pages 129–133)

Objectives (Lesson Focus)

Upon completion of this section, students will be able to:

- Define the terms *rent, interest, profit, bond, stock, dividend,* and *capital gain.*
- Explain how each of these terms relates to the ability firms have to acquire factors of production.
- Explain how the forces of demand and supply set the price of stock on a stock exchange.

Preparation (Instruction: Pre-teaching—Vocabulary or Activity)

1. Discussion Introduce this section by listing the amounts of money necessary to start various franchise businesses. The following were advertised in the *Wall Street Journal* on 7/30/87.

Type of Franchise	Minimum Investment
a photocopy business	$ 16,000
a submarine sandwich restaurant	$ 29,900
an artist supply store	$ 50,000
a tutoring service	$ 70,000
a hamburger restaurant	$250,000
an equipment rental business	$250,000

Ask your students how they would go about raising the money necessary to go into these or other businesses.

2. The Personal Narrative The Personal Narrative in Section D continues the story of Rita and Joshua. In this section the couple decide to expand their business but experience difficulty in raising the necessary money. They do not have sufficient funds of their own, Rita's father is unwilling to lend them more, and they are turned down for a large enough loan by a bank. Eventually they agree to form a corporation and sell a controlling interest in their business to other people.

The Narrative demonstrates the financial limitations of single proprietorships and partnerships. It also shows the ability of the corporate form of business organization to gather money through the sale of stock and bonds.

Teaching Suggestions (Modeling/Guided Practice)

1. Tell your students to assume that they are loan officers for a local bank. Assign them to write two paragraphs.

    a. In the first paragraph they should choose a local business that they would be willing to lend $500,000. They should explain three different reasons that cause them to believe that the firm is worthy of the loan.

    b. In the second paragraph they should choose a different local business that they would not be willing to lend $500,000. They should explain three different reasons that cause them to believe the firm is not worthy of the loan.

2. Many businesses choose to rent equipment rather than buy it. Discuss the advantages and disadvantages of renting an expensive computer. These would include:

    Advantages

    a. lower monthly payments
    b. can't get "stuck" owning out-of-date equipment
    c. allows firm to use its money for other things

    Disadvantages

    a. don't own equipment at end of rental period.
    b. may not have the same tax advantages
    c. may cost more in the long run

3. Discuss the advantages and disadvantages of allowing a controlling interest of a privately held corporation, or a proprietorship or partnership to be bought by others. How much is it worth to be able to make business decisions for yourself? How much freedom does any business really have, considering the ideas of the invisible hand and consumer sovereignty?

Lesson Checkpoint

Text: Self-Check, text page 133
        Answers

1. Rent and interest are both payments for the use of resources that are owned by someone else.

2. Larger, established businesses are considered to have a lower risk than smaller, newer businesses.

3. When the price of a type of stock goes up, this indicates a situation in which more people want to own the stock and fewer people want to sell it.

Follow-up Assignments (Independent Practice/Extension/Homework)

1. Text: Applying What You Have Learned, text page 133
           Answers

    Rita and Joshua considered borrowing money from a bank (or from Paul, Rita's father) or by forming a corporation and selling stock. They wanted more money so they could buy additional factors of production to expand their business. They were particularly interested in obtaining more capital (tools, equipment, etc.), and labor (workers for new restaurants).

2. Teacher's Resource Binder: Critical Thinking Activity, Chapter 5 (answers in Binder).

Section Evaluation

Self-Check, text page 133

Understanding Economics, questions 4–6
(Chapter 5 Review, text pages 135–137)

ADDITIONAL MATERIALS FOR CHAPTER 5

Chapter Evaluation

Teacher's Resource Binder: Chapter 5 Quiz

Reteaching and Extension

See the *Teacher's Resource Binder* and the *Student Activity Guide* for additional handouts and activities for Chapter 5.

TEACHER'S BIBLIOGRAPHY FOR CHAPTER 5

Economic Sources

Gordon, Sanford D., and Dawson, George G. *Introductory Economics*, 6th ed. Lexington, Mass.: D. C. Heath, Inc., 1987. Chapters 4, 5, and 6 explain in simple fashion business organizations, antitrust action, and the firm's costs and prices.

Heilbroner, Robert L., and Galbraith, James K., II. *The Economic Problem*. Englewood Cliffs, N.J.: Prentice-Hall, Inc., 1987. See pages 70–73 and 85–90 for a short description of the organizational structure of business and business trends.

Love, John F. *McDonald's: Behind the Arches*. New York: Bantam, 1986. A good case study of a successful enterprise that shows the importance of the entrepreneur as well as the corporation.

Sobel, Robert, and Sicilia, David B. *The Entrepreneurs: an American Adventure*. Boston: Houghton Mifflin, 1986. Describes many innovations in American business.

References for Additional Teaching Strategies

How a Business Operates. Four film strips with cassettes, reproducible worksheets, and a study guide that help students learn about business costs, profits, finance, and productivity. Social Studies School Service, P.O. Box 802, Culver City, CA 90230-9983.

Niss, James; Brenneke, Judith; and Clow, John. *Basic Business and Consumer Education*. New York: Joint Council on Economic Education, 1979. Lesson 6 for costs, prices, and profits; Lesson 7 on production costs; Lesson 8 on the role of advertising.

CHAPTER 5 REVIEW ANSWERS

Building Your Vocabulary   (text page 136)

1. variable costs
2. stock
3. limited life
4. single proprietorship
5. corporation
6. partnership
7. dividend
8. limited liability
9. unlimited life
10. fixed costs
11. rent
12. capital gain
13. average fixed cost
14. interest
15. bond
16. prime rate
17. unlimited liability

Understanding Economics   (text page 136)

1. a. Corporations offer limited liability. Owners of stock risk no more than the value of their investment in the stock of the firm.

   b. Corporations are better able to raise funds through the sale of stock and bonds.

   c. Corporations have unlimited life: if an

individual stock owner dies, the firm will continue to function.

2. Students could choose any number of different firms. Their lists should demonstrate a knowledge of the difference between fixed and variable costs.

3. The average cost of raising a child in a large family could be lower than the cost for raising only one child because the same items of furniture and clothing can be used more than just one time.

4. Corporations must pay interest on their bonds regardless of whether the firm earns a profit. Also, if the firm fails, bondholders have call on the assets of the firm before any of the stockholders.

5. A rich person might choose to buy stock instead of a bond because he or she is better able to afford a risk. If the firm does well, the value of its stock could increase and it could pay large dividends.

6. Very profitable firms are the best credit risks and therefore are best able to borrow money at the lower interest rate.

Thinking Critically About Economics
(text pages 136–137)

1. *Firm A* should be a partnership because the lawyers would benefit from sharing the costs of a law library, computer, secretary, and assistants. It would be difficult to sell stock in such a firm. *Firm B* should be a corporation because it will require large investments that could only be made by many owners. *Firm C* should be a single proprietorship because it will not require large investments and the owner will take responsibility for its operation.

2. If John sells camping equipment as well, he would be able to distribute the cost of his rent to more products. This would lower his average fixed cost per item and would probably increase his profit per item sold.

3. I sell 10 bicycles a day for $110 each so I have a total revenue of $1,100 a day. My costs are now $50 in fixed costs and $80 in variable costs for each of the 10 bicycles. This totals $850. I am making $250 a day in profit now.

   If I lowered my price to $100, I would sell 20 bicycles a day to take in $2,000 in total revenue. My costs would be the $50 in fixed costs plus $80 multiplied by 20 bicycles in variable costs for a total of $1,650. I would then earn a profit of $350. Therefore, I should lower my price.

4. a. Sharon could try to borrow the money she needs from a bank. Banks, however, may be unwilling to make large loans to such a small firm.

   b. Sharon could try to find private investors who would either loan her the money or become partners. This would be relatively difficult to accomplish and could dilute her control.

   c. Sharon could form a corporation and sell stock. This would be a relatively difficult process and one for which she would probably need legal help. It could also require her to give up control of the firm if she sold more than fifty percent of the stock to other people.

5. If the firm Barbara has invested in continues to grow rapidly, it may earn large profits in the future. This should increase the number of people who want to own its stock. The price of the stock would then go up and Barbara could sell her stock for a capital gain.

Special Skills Projects   (text page 137)

1. These interviews should clearly indicate the disadvantages and advantages of each form of business organization.

2. This project is so extensive that it might be better to assign it to groups of students

who could do it together. Point out the division of labor that this allows.

3. It might be better to choose stocks in firms that have local plants or offices. If students' parents work for any of the firms, they may have information that would be helpful for this project. Point out that the use of "insider" information in buying and selling stock is against the law.

CHAPTER 6

Perfect and Imperfect Competition (text pages 140–171)

SECTION A.   Perfect Competition (text pages 143–146)

Objectives   (Lesson Focus)

Upon completion of this section, students will be able to:

- Recognize and explain the characteristics of perfect competition.

- Explain how the market acts as a regulator of the economy through its competitive forces.

- Explain possible advantages offered by diversification in a competitive market.

- Identify possible dangers of having too much competition.

Preparation   (Instruction: Pre-teaching— Vocabulary or Activity)

1. Discussion   Introduce this section by asking your students what it is like to try to get a date with the most popular boy/girl in school. In effect they would be in competition with many other students who have the same idea. They would have to be nicer, more attractive, or have a better car to succeed. If they said something wrong, they might never get another chance.

Explain that running a business in a competitive market is much the same. Like popular students, customers have their choice. They may patronize many different firms who all want their business. Firms must offer the best service, quality products, and lower prices. Even if a customer buys from a store once, there is no guarantee that he/she will buy there again in the future. Running a business in a competitive market is not an easy task.

2. The Personal Narrative   The Personal Narrative in Section A describes a business in a market that is close to perfect competition. The subject of the Narrative owns a filling station and convenience store on a busy highway near many other stores that sell similar products. His customers shop largely according to prices, which he must therefore keep low. He has diversified into other types of products and cut his costs in an attempt to improve his profits.

The Narrative demonstrates the difficulty of running a firm in a competitive market. It also shows the benefits of competition for the consumer.

Teaching Suggestions   (Modeling/Guided Practice)

1. Ask your students to identify a type of business that they think they could actually start and own by themselves. List several of these on the board. You should find that most of them are in markets that are quite competitive. Point this out to your students. Firms that individuals can start tend to be quite small and require limited financial resources. Therefore, many people who want to go into business will go into these types of businesses. This causes strong competition, forcing firms to charge low prices and earn small profits. Most business failures

occur among small businesses in competitive markets.

2. Use Discussion Topic 10 from the *Teacher's Resource Binder* to show some of the effects of high profits in a competitive economy.

3. Most fast-food restaurants are very competitive. Assign your students to survey prices at different local hamburger or pizza restaurants. They should find that the prices are almost the same. Discuss their findings in class. Can they explain any differences in price in terms of quality, location, or advertising?

Lesson Checkpoint

Text: Self-Check, text page 146
      Answers

1. Customers look for the firms that offer the lowest prices.

2. Diversification can add products for which there is less competition and can also reduce average fixed costs.

3. Too much competition can reduce firms' abilities to accumulate enough wealth to invest in research and new technology and may also reduce firms' abilities to survive a downturn in the economy.

Follow-up Assignments   (Independent Practice/Extension/Homework)

Text: Applying What You Have Learned, text page 146
      Answers

a. If it costs little to start a particular type of business, there can be many of them which will increase competition.

b. If it takes limited skill and training

to run a business, then many people would be able to operate such firms which will increase competition.

c. If it requires few employees to run a business, then it would require less money to operate such businesses, thus allowing more firms to be in competition.

d. If it is easy to buy necessary resources for a business, then many people would be able to run such businesses which would increase competition.

Section Evaluation

Self-Check, text page 146
Understanding Economics, questions 1 and 2 (Chapter 6 Review, text pages 168–170)

SECTION B.   Monopolies (text pages 147–151)

Objectives   (Lesson Focus)

Upon completion of this section, students will be able to:

- Identify and explain the basic characteristics of perfect monopoly, monopolistic competition, oligopoly, and natural monopoly.

- Recognize and explain the relationship between monopoly-like powers and the four-firm concentration ratio.

Preparation   (Instruction: Pre-teaching— Vocabulary or Activity)

1. Discussion   Introduce this section by telling your students the following story:

Once upon a time in a faraway land, a starving artist named Raphael lived in great poverty. Although he was very poor, he was happy because he liked to paint. He was sure he would succeed if he kept trying.

One day he met a beautiful young princess who fell in love with him because he was pure and honest. The people of the kingdom loved the princess, and because she loved Raphael they bought his paintings, although they were really quite awful. Raphael, however, misunderstood the situation. He thought he had been "discovered" at last. He believed that it was he who the people loved. He raised his prices and spent the money on himself. He acted like he was the king. Soon the princess realized that Raphael had become conceited and greedy so she went away. No one wanted to buy his paintings anymore. Raphael could not pay his bills and died in a debtors' prison.

Help your students understand how the story of Raphael relates to the characteristics of a monopoly. When the princess loved Raphael, he had a monopoly because no one else could paint pictures and be loved by the princess too. He was able to raise prices and make large profits. However, there was a limit to how much he could charge. When he showed himself to be greedy, the princess—and then his customers—decided to do without him and his paintings.

Firms with monopoly-like power can set their own prices and often earn large profits. But if they charge too much, they invite either competition or the substitution of other products by their customers. There are limits to a monopoly's power.

2. The Personal Narrative   The Personal Narrative in Section B describes a business in a market that is almost a pure monopoly. The subject of the Narrative owns the only filling station within 20 miles of a small town in Nebraska. His customers have no realistic alternative to buying his products. As a result, he is able to charge a higher price than more competitive firms in other locations. On the other hand, he is afraid of encouraging competition and does not exploit his market power excessively. He is careful to provide quality service and to keep up with new innovations.

The Narrative demonstrates the advantages of running a firm that has monopoly-like power. It also shows that there are limits on monopoly powers and that customers can benefit from these powers in some ways.

Teaching Suggestions   (Modeling/Guided Practice)

1. Many people believe that the telephone company has or had a pure monopoly. This is not quite true. The telephone is only one of many ways to communicate over a distance. Ask your students to help you make a list of other ways to communicate. Alternatives include telegrams, the mail, carrier pigeons, driving there, smoke signals, tom-toms, etc. Although the telephone company did not have a pure monopoly, it could have set very high prices if the government had allowed this. Ask your students why this is so. Are any of the alternatives to the telephone as quick and easy? Do the alternatives to the telephone represent meaningful competition? Why are government regulations of telephone rates necessary?

2. Most school cafeterias have a form of monopoly. Students usually must either buy food in the cafeteria or bring their lunch from home. Ask your students to take a survey among themselves and their friends:

   How many eat cafeteria food for their lunch?
   How many would eat their lunch elsewhere if they had a choice?

How much do they feel the cafeteria food is really worth?
What do they believe the cafeteria would do if it had any real competition?

Discuss the results of the survey in class. You should point out that most school cafeterias are supported in part from taxes and therefore charge less than private restaurants can afford to charge.

3. Assign your students to cut out advertisements from newspapers that try to convince them to buy a product *without mentioning price*. Discuss the ads in class and classify them as having been placed by firms that are in competition, monopolistic competition, oligopoly, or natural monopoly. It is likely that the majority will be from firms in monopolistic competition. Explain this is because these firms are trying to make a distinction in the minds of the consumer between their products and similar products.

Lesson Checkpoint

Text: Self-Check, text page 151
Answers

1. The factors include the possibility that high prices will cause low sales and an increased fixed cost per item; high prices may also encourage competition or the substitution of other products by the consumer.

2. An imperfect market exists when businesses are large enough to have some—but not complete—control over the prices they can charge customers.

3. Three types of imperfect markets are monopolistic competition, oligopoly, and natural monopoly.

Follow-up Assignments   (Independent Practice/Extension/Homework)

Text: Applying What You Have Learned, text page 151
Answers

a. Property values and services provided by the government in rural areas are smaller. Therefore, property taxes tend to be lower.

b. Insurance would be less costly because there is usually less crime in rural areas.

c. It may be easier to find people who are willing to work for lower wages in a rural area because the cost of living is also likely to be lower.

d. The original building will be less costly in a rural area because of lower wage rates for construction and lower property values for the land on which it is located.

Section Evaluation

Self-Check, text page 151
Understanding Economics, questions 3, 4 and 5 (Chapter 6 Review, text pages 168–170)

SECTION C.   Combinations and Big Business (text pages 153–157)

Objectives   (Lesson Focus)

Upon completion of this section, students will be able to:

- Explain the difference between horizontal and vertical combinations.
- Explain the respective advantages offered by horizontal and vertical combinations.
- Describe how large firms are able to either help or harm their customers' interests.

Preparation   (Instruction: Pre-teaching—Vocabulary or Activity)

1. Discussion Introduce this section by asking your students to list all the reasons they might choose to shop at one store instead of another. Possible reasons would include price, selection, quality, friendly service, availability of repairs, and reputation.

Then help your students identify specific stores that compete in the area of their school. Be sure that some are locally owned, and others are parts of large chains.

Are some of the reasons identified by your students more often associated with large chain stores, while others are associated with local firms? What effect do your students believe competition between the large and small firms has on the owners of the small firms?

2. The Personal Narrative The Personal Narrative in Section C describes how the owner of a small independent store is affected by competition with a much larger chain store. The subject of the Narrative owns a hardware store and prides himself on providing quality products and service. However, he is unable to match the low prices of a new discount store.

The Narrative shows students the problems that can result for the owners of small firms when they compete with larger firms. It emphasizes the fact that low prices are not the only benefits firms can offer their customers.

Teaching Suggestions (Modeling/Guided Practice)

1. Explain that many small stores have joined associations which are able to provide advantages similar to those of larger firms. These associations can advertise more efficiently, distribute goods quickly, and buy products in quantity to cut costs. One example of this is the Independent Grocer's Association, which is made up of many small grocery stores. What other businesses can your students identify that have done the same? Others include independent drug stores, hardware stores, and auto parts stores. These organizations offer advantages that are similar to those of a horizontal combination.

2. Some of your students may have part-time jobs in large chain stores. Ask them to explain what they do if a customer brings back a product that does not work. Do they feel that they are qualified to explain many of the products they sell? Ask them about the speed with which employees come and go at their store. Is the store able to keep good people? What do the answers to these questions mean to the quality of customer service and satisfaction at a large chain store? If other students work in a small local store, ask them the same questions and see how their answers compare with the answers of the students who work in chain stores.

3. Emphasize the fact that big is not necessarily bad. Large firms may be much more efficient than similar smaller firms. This efficiency may result in lower prices and high quality. If large firms offered no advantages, people would realize it and stop buying from them. The fact that many people continue to buy from large businesses supports the idea that they are making an important contribution to our economic success.

4. Assign your students to survey the prices of several products at local hardware stores and at large chain discount stores. Have them report their findings to the class. How significant is the difference in prices? Help your students find the average percentage difference. Would your students choose to shop at the small local store or at the discount store?

Lesson Checkpoint

Text: Self-Check, text page 157
Answers

1. When one type of business grows, there is a good chance that some other type of business will shrink or fail.
2. A horizontal combination is a joining of firms that do the same thing.
3. Vertical combinations are often able to sell their products for less because they can control most of their costs of production.

Follow-up Assignments   (Independent Practice/Extension/Homework)

Text: Applying What You Have Learned, text page 157
Answers

1. Possible answers include:

   a. There could be no one to repair many products.
   b. There could be less competition so the other store could increase price.
   c. There could be a further decline in the quality offered by the discount store.
   d. There could be less choice in the type of products people could buy.
   e. There could be a reduction in the number of good jobs offered in the community.

2. The advertisements should include reference to things like:

   a. quality service
   b. convenient hours
   c. quick repairs
   d. wide choice in products

Section Evaluation

Self-Check, text page 157
Understanding Economics, question 6
   (Chapter 6 Review, text pages 168–170)

SECTION D.   Advantages and Disadvantages of Big Business (text pages 158–161)

Objectives   (Lesson Focus)

Upon completion of this section, students will be able to:

- Identify and explain several examples of economies of scale.

- Identify and explain several examples of diseconomies of scale.

Preparation   (Instruction: Pre-teaching— Vocabulary or Activity)

1. Discussion   Introduce this section by showing students a copy of a mail-order catalog from a large retailer like Sears or Penny's. Ask them why they would or would not like to shop from such a catalog. Point out that people who lived in rural areas 50 to 70 years ago often did most of their shopping from mail-order catalogs because there were few stores near their homes. Local stores they could go to stocked few items and often had higher prices. Help your students list reasons that allowed the mail-order firms to offer more selection and lower prices than local firms. Ask your students what dangers there may have been in shopping from mail-order catalogs.

   Most of the differences your students identify will be related to the size of each firm's market. A large firm can stock more items and sell at lower prices because it sells many more products. It can also afford to try new ideas that smaller firms could not risk. On the other hand, the local firm can provide more personal service. If a product is defective, it does not have to be returned through the mail.

Point out that many of these same characteristics are associated with large and small firms today. Economists call them economies and diseconomies of scale.

2. The Personal Narrative The Personal Narrative in Section D describes how an individual customer is affected by competition between a small independent store and a much larger chain store. The subject of the Narrative used to shop at a small local hardware store where he received personal service but felt prices were high. He now frequents a large chain discount store where he pays lower prices but receives less personal service.

The Narrative shows students the trade-offs customers make when they choose to shop at different stores. It emphasizes the fact that low prices are only one of many things firms can offer their customers.

Teaching Suggestions (Modeling/Guided Practice)

1. Organize a debate in your class. Select one group of students who will represent a large drug chain that wants to open a new store in your neighborhood. A second group will represent the owners of a small, locally owned drugstore. The question to be debated is whether or not the city council should rezone a vacant lot from residential to commercial so the chain store will have a place to build. Students should center their arguments on what the store has to offer their community, and what it will cost the community and the owners of the local store. What are the advantages and disadvantages of the large store to the community?

2. Point out that many new innovations are very expensive. One example is diagnostic electronic devices that are used to find and analyze problems in cars. These machines cost many thousands of dollars and take special training to be used properly. Today's cars have become so complicated that many problems cannot be repaired without such machines. Although large service centers have diagnostic devices, many small private garages cannot afford to buy them or to train people to use them. Discuss why expensive innovations may lead to small firms either being put out of business, or forced to grow, or to merge with other firms.

3. Assign your students to ask their parents and other adults how they have been affected by the breakup of the phone company. Also have them ask how many long-distance calls each person makes. Combine the results of the surveys on the chalkboard and try to draw conclusions concerning how people feel about the dissolution of the phone company. Can your students find a difference between the opinions of business owners and of people who only have home phones? People who make many long distance calls should have benefited from lower long distance rates.

Lesson Checkpoint

Text: Self-Check, text page 161
      Answers

1. The importance of economies of scale is evidenced by so many firms growing larger.

2. Rockefeller said that Standard Oil's profits were the result of efficiency.

3. The courts divided Standard Oil into several smaller companies in 1914.

Follow-up Assignments (Independent Practice/Extension/Homework)

1. Text: Applying What You Have Learned, text page 161
   Answers

   Possible answers include:

   a. lack of choice or lower quality
   b. no service department to repair products
   c. no knowledgeable salespeople
   d. impersonal service

2. Teacher's Resource Binder: Critical Thinking Activity, Chapter 6 (answers in Binder).

Section Evaluation

Self-Check, text page 161
Understanding Economics, question 7
   (Chapter 6 Review, text pages 168–170)

SECTION E.   The Government's Role in Competition (text pages 162–166)

Objectives (Lesson Focus)
Upon completion of this section, students will be able to:

- Define and explain the significance of workable competition.
- Describe how government antitrust policy tries to achieve workable competition.

Preparation (Instruction: Pre-teaching— Vocabulary or Activity)

1. Discussion   Introduce this section by asking students if they would rather attend a large or small college or vocational school after they graduate from high school. There are some state-sponsored schools with as many as 50,000 students. Some private schools have 250 or fewer students. What advantages and disadvantages are associated with the size of a school?

Large schools may offer more specialized classes and equipment. Small schools may provide more individualized instruction. One responsibility of state education authorities is to see that their colleges do not become too large to provide quality education.

Explain that many of the advantages and disadvantages of size in schools are also applicable to businesses. It is the responsibility of the government's antitrust division to protect the interests of the people by balancing the advantages of bigness with the dangers of monopoly power. Any time a decision is made, there is a trade-off between the costs and benefits of size.

2. The Personal Narrative   The Personal Narrative in Section E describes the effect of government-approved dissolutions and mergers on consumers. The subject of the Narrative has received a seven-page phone bill that he does not understand. The point is made that the break-up of the phone company was accomplished with government oversight. Similar events in the airline industry and in military contracting are mentioned.

The Narrative shows students that there is a trade-off when the government allows dissolutions or mergers. In many cases some people gain while others lose. Making the best choice for all is a difficult task.

Teaching Suggestions   (Modeling/Guided Practice)

1. In 1986 and 1987 there was a rapid increase in the number of near misses between aircraft. The rate increased by almost 30 percent in the first six months of 1987 alone. Some people said deregulation of the airline industry led to this problem. Discuss this issue in the context of what has happened since 1987. Was

deregulation a good idea? Has it led to too many flights and lax controls? What have the costs and benefits been in terms of passenger safety?

2. Tell your students the following story. This story is not far from that of the Lockheed Corporation in the early 1970s. In that case the government did guarantee a billion-dollar bank loan that saved the firm from bankruptcy.

There is a very large firm that is in danger of going bankrupt. The firm's problems are largely the result of poor planning and management. It has also been suggested that some of the firm's workers have been paid too much and have been lazy.

The firm employs over 60,000 workers. It has an annual payroll of almost $2 billion. The firm's employees pay over $700 million in taxes to federal, state, and local governments each year. If the firm closed, these taxes would not be paid and former workers would receive many millions of dollars in benefits from the government.

The firm is a major supplier of government military equipment. If it failed, important military projects would be slowed down. Failure would also reduce competition within the military equipment industry.

The firm has asked the government to help it get a $1 billion bank loan. The owners of many small firms have protested, claiming that if they had been poor managers the government would not have helped them.

Should the government help the firm get the loan? What do your students believe should be done?

Lesson Checkpoint

Text: Self-Check, text page 166
      Answers

1. Such a balance is called workable competition.
2. A firm that is found guilty of violating antitrust laws can be fined or broken up into smaller companies.
3. AT&T was accused of monopolizing telephone service.

Follow-up Assignments   (Independent Practice/Extension/Homework)

Text: Applying What You Have Learned, text page 166
      Answers

The answer to this question will be related to the values of each individual student. Their answers should reflect a reasonable level of thought and logic. There is a trade-off between more government control and individual freedom to run a business. The students' explanations should show an awareness of these trade-offs.

Section Evaluation

Self-Check, text page 166

ADDITIONAL MATERIALS FOR CHAPTER 6

Chapter Evaluation

Teacher's Resource Binder: Chapter Quiz

Reteaching and Extension

See the *Teacher's Resource Binder* and the *Student Activity Guide* for additional handouts and activities for Chapter 6.

TEACHER'S BIBLIOGRAPHY FOR CHAPTER 6

Economics Sources

Adams, Walter, ed. *The Structure of American Industry*, 5th ed. New York: The Macmillan Co., 1977. An excellent analysis of different market structures showing imperfect markets.

Carson, Robert B. *Economic Issues: Alternative Approaches*, 4th ed. New York: St. Martin's Press, 1987. See Issue 4 on "Market Structure: What Should Be Our Policy toward Bigness in Business?" for three contrasting viewpoints.

Clark, J. R., and Veseth, Michael. *Economics: Cost and Choice*. Orlando: Academic Press, 1987. Chapters 18, 19, and 20 cover the basic theory and have excellent illustrations.

Green, Mark, and Berry, John F. *The Challenge of Hidden Profits: Reducing Corporate Bureaucracy and Waste*. New York: Morrow, 1985. Using interviews with executives, this book exposes poor management.

References for Additional Teaching Strategies

Morton, John, et al. *High School Economics Courses*. New York: Joint Council on Economic Education, 1985. See Lesson 12, "When There Isn't Pure Competition," for a lesson plan and handouts.

CHAPTER 6 REVIEW ANSWERS

Building Your Vocabulary   (text page 169)

1. regulatory agency
2. vertical combination
3. perfect competition
4. workable competition
5. oligopoly
6. antitrust policy
7. economies of scale
8. monopolistic competition
9. diversification
10. horizontal combination
11. perfect monopoly
12. diseconomy of scale
13. natural monopoly
14. imperfect competition

Understanding Economics   (text pages 169–170)

1. Small stores often earn small profits because they often have low sales. This means that their fixed costs per item are rather high. To be competitive with larger firms they can be forced to accept a smaller profit margin.

2. Many stores, small stores included, have diversified into selling other types of products. By selling more items, they can reduce their average fixed cost per item sold. This improves their chance of earning a profit.

3. If a store made very high profits, it would encourage other people to open up similar stores in the area. This would result in competition, which would eventually force prices and profits down.

4. Possible answers include:

   a. *Soap.* Advertisers try to convince consumers that there will be more meaning in their lives if they use their particular brand of soap.

   b. *Hair color.* Advertisers try to convince consumers that by coloring their hair with the firm's product they will look younger or more beautiful.

   c. *Pain relievers.* Advertisers try to convince consumers that doctors would really choose the advertised brand of aspirin over some other product if they were lost in the woods.

5. The cost of building a utility can run into the billions of dollars. It would make no sense to spend this amount of money twice to service the same area. No amount of competition could justify such spending.

6. To make a hamburger chain a vertical combination, it would be necessary to join a beef farmer, wheat farmer, potato farmer, baker, dairy, pickle producer, paper product manufacturer, and many other firms that supply hamburger stands together.

7. The following are possible answers:

    a. GM can buy natural resources at lower costs.

    b. GM can advertise and distribute more efficiently.

    c. GM can borrow at lower interest rates.

Thinking Critically About Economics   (text page 170)

1. The following are possible answers:

    a. I could hire a famous person to visit my store and wear my clothes.

    b. I could advertise on TV or on radio.

    c. I could move to a mall with less competition.

2. These three firms illustrate an oligopoly, in that they all operate in the same market and sell the same basic product. Their costs of production are about the same and many of their employees have worked for more than one of the firms. It is not surprising to find them all performing more or less the same functions.

3. Breaking up electric companies into smaller firms would be inefficient because:

    a. the new firms would have to invest in similar equipment.

    b. much of the equipment would be underutilized.

    c. the new firms would have to hire many new workers to service the new equipment.

4. Possible answers showing the advantage of the larger farms include:

    a. The merged farms have the ability to borrow money at lower cost.

    b. The merged farms can afford to buy new, more expensive equipment.

    c. The merged farms should be able to distribute product more efficiently.

Special Skills Projects   (text page 170)

1. Your students will discover that most of these stores sell many products that you would not have found them selling in the past. This demonstrates their diversification.

2. Air fares from the past are likely to be higher if the students go back far enough in time. Deregulation resulted in competition and price wars. Students' answers could vary widely depending on the time they look up the information.

CHAPTER 7

Labor and the Economy: "I Built a Railroad,. . ."(text pages 172–211)

SECTION A.   How Wages are Set (text pages 175–181)

Objectives   (Lesson Focus)

Upon completion of this section, students will be able to:

- Place the labor market as part of the factor market in the circular flow model.
- Explain why the demand for labor, or other factors of production, is a derived demand.
- Identify examples of diminishing marginal productivity.
- Recognize a definition of the labor force participation rate, and explain the relationship between changes in wage rates and the willingness of people to look for work.
- Recognize how the forces of demand and supply for labor result in an equilibrium wage rate.
- Explain the difference between nominal wages and real wages that have been adjusted for inflation.

Preparation   (Instruction: Pre-teaching—Vocabulary or Activity)

1. Discussion   Introduce this section by using Discussion Topic 11 from the *Teacher's Resource Binder* to draw a supply curve for labor based on responses from your students.

2. The Personal Narrative   The Personal Narrative in Section A describes an individual worker who is affected by a decline in his employer's sales. The subject of the Narrative has been laid off due to greater competition in the product market. His employer has suggested that he could have his job back if he and other union members are willing to accept reduced wages. He is faced with the prospect of being forced to take a job that pays less than his old job.

The Narrative demonstrates the relationship between a firm's ability to sell its product and the number of workers it will choose to hire. It shows how workers and employers

are affected by diminishing marginal productivity.

Teaching Suggestions   (Modeling/Guided Practice)

1. Ask your students to read the *help wanted* advertisements from a local newspaper. Tell them to find five different jobs that are frequently advertised. List the jobs they identify on the chalkboard. Can any generalizations be made about the level of skill and training necessary for the jobs listed? Are low- or high-skill workers more in demand?

2. Use Discussion Topic 12 from the *Teacher's Resource Binder* to reinforce the principle of diminishing marginal utility.

3. Discuss the following with your students:
   There is a limited number of people who know how to shoe horses. Ask your students what would happen to the demand for the labor of blacksmiths, and their resultant earnings, if horseback riding became very popular. Discuss how these events would fit into the circular flow model. If the earnings of blacksmiths increased rapidly, what should happen to the number of people who choose to learn this skill? What should happen to the higher earnings of blacksmiths over time?

Lesson Checkpoint

Text: Self-Check, text page 181
  Answers

   1. Natural resources, labor, capital, and entrepreneurship are sold in the factor market.

   2. Diminishing marginal productivity refers to the point where adding more workers results in fewer additional products being produced.

3. At a higher product price, a firm will be willing to hire more workers at the same wage rate.

4. As wage rates increase, more people should want to work.

Follow-up Assignments   (Independent Practice/Extension/Homework)

Text: Applying What You Have Learned, text page 181
Answers

a. At a wage rate of $50, 600 workers would want jobs.

b. At a wage rate of $250, 300 jobs would be available.

c. At a wage rate of $250, there would be a surplus of workers.

d. At a wage rate of $250, there would be a surplus of 300 workers.

e. The equilibrium wage rate in this example is $200.

Section Evaluation

Self-Check, text page 181
Understanding Economics, questions 1 and 2 (Chapter 7 Review, text pages 198–201)

SECTION B.   Labor Unions in the Economy (text pages 182–187)

Objectives   (Lesson Focus)

Upon completion of this section, students will be able to:

- Describe what a labor union is and explain how it attempts to serve its members through collective action.

- Recognize, define, and explain the differences between industrial and craft unions.

- Describe the significance of labor laws, including: The Sherman Antitrust Act of 1890, The Clayton Act of 1914, The National Labor Relations Act of 1935, and The Taft-Hartley Act of 1947.

Preparation   (Instruction: Pre-teaching—Vocabulary or Activity)

1. Discussion   Introduce this section by dividing your class into two groups, one representing the workers at a firm that makes bowling balls, the other representing the owners. Then give the students copies of the story in Discussion Topic 13 from the *Teacher's Resource Binder*.

The group of students representing workers should develop a set of arguments to convince workers to form a union. The group representing the owners should develop a set of reasons why workers should not form a union. The arguments should then be presented to the class as a whole.

2. The Personal Narrative   The Personal Narrative in Section B describes the problems that individual workers could have that might lead them to form unions. The subject of the Narrative works in a cannery to support her family. She feel that her earnings are too low and that her work is dull and dangerous. She has mixed feelings about the possibility of forming a union. On one side, she feels exploited by her employer. On the other, she is afraid a union could cost her the job she needs to support her family.

The Narrative describes the trade-off between costs and benefits that workers consider when they decide whether to organize a union.

Teaching Suggestions   (Modeling/Guided Practice)

Choose two local firms. One should be a large successful firm that employs skilled workers. A pharmaceutical or computer services firm could be a good example. The other firm should be a grocery store or a fast-food restaurant that does not employ highly skilled workers or have a large profit margin. Discuss why workers at the firm firm would probably be more successful in negotiating raises and improved working conditions than those at the second firm. Point out that the workers at the first firm would be more difficult to replace and that the demand for the firm's product is probably relatively inelastic (if the firm raises its price, its sales will not go down much).

Lesson Checkpoint

Text: Self-Check, text page 187
Answers

1. The two basic types of labor unions are craft unions and industrial unions.

2. In accordance with the NLRB, management must negotiate with any union that has organized more than half of the firm's workers.

3. Union membership has fallen since 1960.

Follow-up Assignments   (Independent Practice/Extension/Homework)

Text: Applying What You Have Learned, text page 187
Answers

1. A union might be able to prevent

   a. people being fired the first time they fall asleep.

   b. the firm from hiring new workers.

   c. unsafe working conditions.

   d. low wages.

   e. inadequate benefits for workers who are hurt on the job.

2. The following are possible answers:
   Management might believe that

   a. people should be fired if they fall asleep and cause waste or damage to equipment.

   b. they should be able to hire other workers who are willing to work for relatively low wages.

   c. working conditions are safe if workers take reasonable care in their jobs.

   d. the wages are as much as the firm can afford to pay.

   e. more insurance could only be afforded if workers would accept lower pay.

Section Evaluation

Self-Check, text page 187
Understanding Economics, questions 3 and 4 (Chapter 7 Review, text pages 198–201)

SECTION C.   Labor-Management Relations (text pages 188–192)

Objectives   (Lesson Focus)

Upon completion of this section, students will be able to:

- Define and explain possible steps the government can take to help resolve labor disputes, including mediation, fact-finding, voluntary arbitration, and compulsory arbitration.

- Define terms, including union shop, agency shop, slowdown, boycott, secondary boycott, sit-down strike, strike, picket line, union label, political action committee, lockout, strikebreaker, and relocation.

Preparation   (Instruction: Pre-teaching— Vocabulary or Activity)

1. Discussion   Introduce this section by asking your students to rank each of the following considerations according to their importance. Which ones do your students feel they would be most likely to go on strike for if they were ten years older and had a family to support? (You may want to be more specific about the demands. Suggestions are made in parentheses.)

1. Higher pay _____ (a 10 percent raise)
2. Greater job security _____ (a no layoff guarantee)
3. Better health care _____ (full coverage of all medical bills)
4. Safer working conditions _____ (removal of toxic chemicals from the workplace)
5. Better retirement benefits _____ (full retirement after 30 years regardless of age)

After discussing these demands from a worker's point of view, consider them once more from the owner's point of view. Which ones would the owner be most likely to agree to? Which would be resisted the most?

Discuss how this exercise shows that union-management negotiations may be an adversarial rather than a cooperative process.

2. The Personal Narrative The Personal Narrative for Section C describes the 1986–1987 USX strike from the point of view of one worker and his family. The subject of the Narrative is a young man whose father is on strike against USX. The Narrative explains factors which support the workers' position and the company's point of view.

The Narrative demonstrates the conflict between the needs of a firm's workers and its desire to remain competitive and earn a profit. It shows that compromise may be an alternative to confrontation.

Teaching Suggestions (Modeling/Guided Practice)

1. Tell your students to imagine they are the chairpersons of the board of a large corporation (you may want to identify a specific firm for your class). They have just

agreed to give their workers a 10 percent wage increase. In the long run they feel the increase is in the best interest of the firm and its stockholders. There will be no strike to interfere with business this year. The firm's sales have been good and profits have been high so they can afford to pay the increase. They also believe about 20 percent of the workers can be eliminated over the next few years through the purchase of new equipment. However, the firm's profits will be smaller next year because of the agreement.

Each student should write a letter to the stockholders in which they explain the firm's reasoning behind the settlement. Read several of the better letters in class and discuss their reasoning. (You can do the same exercise with the firm refusing to give the workers a 10 percent increase, thus precipitating a strike.)

2. Discuss why politicians do not like major strikes. Strikes are bad for the country's economy and for people who hold elective offices. Voters may feel their leaders are responsible for problems that result from strikes. Inflation, shortages, layoffs of nonstriking workers, picket-line violence, plant closings, loss of tax revenue, extra government spending for social programs, and loss of foreign markets can all result from major strikes. Students should be aware of the implications of labor unrest for government leaders.

Lesson Checkpoint

Text: Self-Check, text page 192

Answers

1. Right-to-work laws say that workers cannot be required to join or pay a fee to a union if they don't want to.
2. Unions and management negoti-

ate through the process of collective bargaining.

3. Workers lose wages, owners lose profits, government loses tax revenues, and consumers lose the use and benefits of products.

Follow-up Assignments (Independent Practice/Extension/Homework)

1. Text: Applying What You Have Learned, text page 192

    Answers

    Student evaluations of these two arguments depend on their individual values. Their answers should be graded according to how well they are supported with logic and reason.

    Possible arguments from the union's point of view:

    a. They helped the firms through hard times; now their help should be rewarded.

    b. Many firms have returned to profitability and can afford to pay higher wages.

    Possible arguments from the management's point of view:

    a. Current profits should be invested in new equipment, not in higher wages.

    b. The return to profits will disappear if wages go back up.

2. Teacher's Resource Binder: Critical Thinking Activity, Chapter 7 (answers in Binder).

Section Evaluation

Self-Check, text page 192
Understanding Economics, question 5
   (Chapter 7 Review, text pages 198–201)

SECTION D. Minimum Wages and Employment (text pages 193–196)

Objectives (Lesson Focus)

Upon completion of this section, students will be able to:

- Discuss the purposes and possible effects of minimum wage laws.
- Define the term *marginal worker*.

Preparation (Instruction: Pre-teaching— Vocabulary or Activity)

1. **Discussion** Introduce this section by asking students to help make a list of benefits they might receive from a first job. This list could include wages, experience, training, good references, or a chance to work their way into a better job. Ask your students to explain which of these benefits is most important to a young person in the long run. Would they be willing to accept a job that paid poorly if it gave them training in a field they are interested in? Why or why not?

2. **The Personal Narrative** The Personal Narrative in Section D describes the effects of changes in the minimum wage on workers who hold low paying jobs. The subject of the Narrative is a woman who believes an increase in the minimum wage would not increase her earnings but instead would only bring other workers up to the wage rate she worked years to achieve. She resents workers who receive higher wages and better benefits because they belong to unions. She wishes the minimum wage was high enough to make a substantial difference in her own compensation.

   The Narrative demonstrates the problems experienced by workers who hold low-, or minimum-wage jobs. It shows how difficult it would be to support a family on such wages.

Teaching Suggestions (Modeling/Guided Practice)

1. Choose a local business that pays the minimum wage to most of its workers. Ask your students to write a brief essay or discuss in class what they believe the firm would do if the minimum wage was increased by 50 cents an hour. Point out the list of possible reactions in their text on pages 194–195. Read and discuss several of the essays in class.

2. Most workers who earn the minimum wage do not belong to unions. Discuss possible reasons for this lack of organization. Are marginal workers too easy to replace? Do they change jobs too often? Is it because they lack specialized skills? Does it have anything to do with the type of firms they work for? Does organized labor see little point in trying to organize these workers?

   If these workers do not belong to unions, why do unions support higher minimum wages?

Lesson Checkpoint

Text: Self-Check, text page 196
   Answers

   1. Firms that pay wages that are already higher than the minimum wage are not directly affected by increases in the minimum wage.
   2. People who earn the minimum wage and who also have another means of support are called marginal workers.
   3. Some people believe the minimum wage helps to protect workers from exploitation, while others believe the minimum wage reduces employment opportunities for the poor.

Follow-up Assignments (Independent Practice/Extension/Homework)

Text: Applying What You Have Learned, text page 196
   Answers

   1. If the minimum wage were increased to $5 the following would be possible results:

      a. fewer jobs that pay minimum wage
      b. more investment in labor-saving machines
      c. firms that had employed low-skilled workers could go out of business
      d. workers could be expected to do more work

   2. Student answers will vary, but they should provide adequate explanation for their three choices. Possible answers include that the firm could accept a smaller profit; increase prices to their customers; pay no more than minimum wage; lay off some workers and make those who remain do more work; purchase labor-saving equipment so they can lay off workers; replace low-skill workers with higher-skilled, more productive workers; or simply close down.

Section Evaluation

Self-Check, text page 196
Thinking Critically About Economics, question 6 (Chapter 7 Review, text pages 198–201)

ADDITIONAL MATERIALS FOR CHAPTER 7

Chapter Evaluation

Teacher's Resource Binder: Chapter Quiz

Reteaching and Extension

See the *Teacher's Resource Binder* and the *Student Activity Guide* for additional handouts and activities for Chapter 7.

TEACHER'S BIBLIOGRAPHY FOR CHAPTER 7

Economics Sources

Carlson, Barbara M., and McEnrue, Mary P. "Eliminating the Gender-Based Earning Gap: Two Alternatives," in Reuben Slesinger and Glen Beeson, eds., *Economics 87/88 Annual Edition*. Guilford, CT: The Dushkin Publishing Group, Inc., 1987. Originally published in *Business Horizons*, this article examines the differential in wages for men and women and suggests strategies for reducing the gap.

Freeman, Richard B., and Medoff, James L. *What Do Unions Do?*. New York: Basic Books, Inc., 1984. A straight-forward presentation of unions, including some of their recent problems.

Marshall, Roy, and Rungeling, Brian. *The Role of Unions in the American Economy*, 2nd ed. New York: Joint Council on Economic Education, 1984. A brief history of the labor union movement with emphasis on past and present problems.

Rees, Albert. *The Economics of Work and Pay*. New York: Harper and Row, 1979. Analyzes the impact of demand and supply on wages. Also presents macroeconomic aspects of the labor market.

Supple, Terry. "The Coming Labor Shortage," in Reuben Slesinger and Glen Beeson, eds., *Economics 87/88 Annual Edition*. Guilford, CT: The Dushkin Publishing Group, Inc., 1987. Originally printed in *American Demographics*, this article shows that with the declining birthrate, the United States may face a serious labor shortage in the years ahead.

References for Additional Teaching Strategies

One Hundred Years of American Labor, 1881–1981. Washington, D.C.: American Federation of Labor and Congress of Industrial Organizations, 1981. A forty-page pamphlet on the history of the American Labor movement.

The National Economy and Trade. Washington, D.C.: American Federation of Labor and Congress of Industrial Organizations, 1986. A 33-page summary of AFL-CIO Policy Recommendations for 1986.

The Management Position

What to Do When the Union Knocks. Washington, D.C.: Chamber of Commerce of the U.S., 1975. Advice to businesses that want to keep the unions out.

CHAPTER 7 REVIEW ANSWERS

Building Your Vocabulary   (text pages 199–200)

Sections A & B

1. injunction
2. diminishing marginal productivity
3. closed shop
4. National Labor Relations Act
5. craft union
6. industrial union
7. equilibrium wage rate
8. Clayton Act
9. right-to-work law
10. derived demand
11. Taft-Hartley Act
12. marginal physical product
13. labor force participation rate
14. money wages
15. real wages
16. diminishing returns
17. labor unions

Sections C & D

18. lockout
19. strike
20. compulsory arbitration
21. Fair Labor Standards Act
22. sit-down strike
23. relocation
24. mediation
25. voluntary arbitration
26. agency shop
27. political action committee
28. marginal workers
29. wildcat strike
30. slowdown
31. picket line
32. union label
33. strikebreaker
34. minimum wage
35. union ship
36. collective bargaining
37. boycott

Understanding Economics   (text pages 200–201)

1. If the saw only requires two workers to operate it, a third worker will only give the two current workers a chance to rest. This will increase production but only by a limited amount. The third worker did not add as much to production as the second worker did. This demonstrates the principle of diminishing marginal productivity.

2. If a firm is suddenly able to charge more for its product, it will find that its workers are worth more and the firm will be willing to not only hire additional workers but also pay them a higher wage.

3. Workers in a car wash are probably low skilled and easy to replace. Aircraft engineers are high-skilled workers and difficult to replace. The aircraft firm is probably more profitable than the car wash. The aircraft workers are therefore in a better position to demand and receive higher wages.

4. If there was an extended rail strike that was harming the national interests, the President could request an injunction from a federal court that would require the workers to return to work for up to 80 days. During this time the federal government would attempt to help the parties reach a settlement through mediation.

5. Facts that I as mediator would want to know before suggesting a solution would include:

    a. what similar workers are paid elsewhere
    b. what fringe benefits the workers receive
    c. what profit the firm makes
    d. what the rate of inflation has been
    e. if the firm could raise its prices
    f. if the workers have been or could be more productive
    g. what investments in new machinery have been or could be made
    h. what wage increases have been given to workers in past contracts

Thinking Critically About Economics (text page 201)

1. Workers who would be harmed by the new equipment would include:

    a. production workers who lost their jobs
    b. people who had maintained the old equipment
    c. workers at firms that sold to the workers who lost their jobs

Workers who would benefit from the new equipment would include:

a. workers who build the new equipment

b. workers who maintain the new equipment

c. workers who sell to the people who gain jobs from the new equipment

2. Reasons to accept concessionary contracts could include:

a. greater job security

b. opportunity for firm to invest in new equipment

c. chance to receive greater income at some future time

3. A right-to-work law could make it more difficult for a union to organize workers for the following possible reasons:

a. Some workers might choose not to join or support the union.

b. Some workers might be afraid that the union could not protect them.

c. There might be more arguments between workers who joined the union and those who did not join.

4. Possible reasons for union membership decline include the following:

a. Some workers may feel unions reduce the number of jobs available.

b. Some workers may feel unions have been unresponsive to their needs.

c. Many former union members have lost their jobs.

5. Owners might use a lockout if they felt that wage concessions could be won by doing so. When sales are low, owners have less to lose by closing down. In a recession, workers may not have enough savings to stay off work for very long.

6. *In Favor:* A lower minimum wage would allow young workers the opportunity to gain experience so that they could get a better job some time in the future. *Against:* A lower minimum wage would only allow employers to take advantage of young workers and to hire fewer older workers.

Special Skills Projects   (text page 201)

1. In general you should find that students whose parents are industrial workers are more likely to be organized in a union. Most students will hold the same points of view concerning unions as their parents. If these ideas are different, it can lead to spirited class discussions.

2. It is likely that union leaders will talk less of money and more of security than they would have ten years ago.

3. The perceptions of the role of unions held by employers is likely to be quite different from those views held by union officials. You may want to discuss the conflict between these points of view and what this can do to the negotiation process.

PART 2 REVIEW ANSWERS

Understanding Economic Concepts   (text pages 205–206)

1. The answer is provided as an example in the text.

2. The number of products a firm sells should increase if the price of similar products goes up. Customers will *substitute* the firm's product for the similar one that is more expensive. This change in one of the *determinants of demand* will cause demand for the firm's product to increase.

3. If a firm pays its workers a higher wage it will have higher *costs of production*, which will cause it to *supply* fewer products if it

is not able to increase the price it charges.

4. If a firm produces more products than it can sell at its current price, it will have a *surplus* of its product. It will probably lower its price to the *equilibrium price*, where the quantity of the product that is demanded will be equal to the quantity the firm is willing to supply. At this lower price, the surplus will be eliminated.

5. Consumers distribute their spending among many different types of products because of *diminishing marginal utility*. As they acquire additional items of a particular type, each one has less value. They are able to receive greater value by buying other types of products.

6. In capitalism firms produce products that consumers buy because it is impossible to earn a profit from producing a product no one wants. The idea that consumers determine what products are produced and offered for sale is called *consumer sovereignty*.

7. The need for the government to provide *consumer protection* has grown over the years because our economic system and the products we buy have become much more complex.

8. Most large firms are corporations because they are able to raise the large amounts of money they need through the sale of *stocks* and *bonds*. Single proprietorships and partnerships are not able to gather money in these ways.

9. Many firms would like to increase the number of products they manufacture or sell to reduce their *average fixed cost*. This practice should reduce their cost per item produced and improve their chance of earning a profit.

10. The owner of corporate stock may earn money when the firm pays a part of its profits to the stockholders in *dividends*. Money may also be earned from a *capital gain* when the value of the stock increases and the owner sells the stock for more than the purchase price.

11. Many large firms have been formed from small firms being joined together. When firms that produce the same product join together, it is called a *horizontal combination*. When firms that provide different steps in the process of producing a single product join together, it is called a *vertical combination*.

12. Some firms require such large capital investments that it would be inefficient to have more than one in any area. These firms are called *natural monopolies*. Public utilities are examples of such firms and are usually regulated by an agency of the government so they cannot take advantage of their customers.

13. The government of the United States uses its antitrust policy to try to create *workable competition*, an attempt to achieve the best trade-off between the advantages of industrial size and those of competition.

14. As firms hire additional workers they will reach a point where extra workers add progressively smaller amounts to production. This fact is called *diminishing marginal productivity*, and it results from the limited resources available for additional workers to use.

15. The government has frequently become involved in labor/management negotiations or the collective bargaining process. This involvement has taken several forms. In *mediation* the government provides a neutral party who listens to both sides and suggests a solution. In *voluntary arbitration* the two sides allow the

neutral party to set the contract or conditions of employment. When there is *compulsory arbitration*, the two sides are required by law to allow the neutral party to set the contract.

Writing About Economics   (text pages 206–207)

1. Students should understand the need firms have to reduce their *average fixed costs* by increasing the number of items they sell. One way this can be accomplished is by providing customers with additional information through *informative advertising*. This advertising may increase the demand for the firm's product by changing customer tastes (a determinant of demand) for the product.

2. Students should understand how *persuasive advertising* may be used to influence consumer tastes. They should demonstrate an appreciation of the trade-offs between freedom of choice and *consumer protection* that are made when the government regulates advertising. Students should finally address the idea of the *invisible hand*, which suggests that a firm which does not charge reasonable prices for quality products will eventually lose its customers and fail.

3. Students should understand the firm's need to convince its customers that its product is superior to other similar goods. If the firm accomplishes this distinction through *informative advertising*, it will be an example of a firm in *monopolistic competition*, because the firm will possess a monopoly over its name and reputation rather than over its type of product.

4. Students should understand the trade-offs that must be made in implementing *antitrust policy*. When *horizontal combina-*

tions are created, the new, larger firms may be able to take advantage of *economies of scale* and become more efficient. However, they might abuse their economic power. The government tries to create *workable competition*, in which the best features of size and competition are achieved.

Discussing Economics   (text pages 207–208)

1. Students should identify the issue(s) that are involved in a law that would require the use of motorcycle helmets. One possible issue is the trade-off between personal freedom and public responsibility to care for individuals who are injured in motorcycle accidents. Students should clearly state whether or not they would support such a law. They should clearly explain the costs and benefits associated with such a law and explain why they believe their point of view is correct.

2. Students should identify the issue(s) that are involved in passing the cost of unfinished nuclear power projects on to customers. One possible issue is the fairness of requiring the individual stockholders of the power company to pay the cost through reduced dividends or the possible failure of the firm. Other possible issues relate to what degree and in what way the owners of government-regulated, natural monopolies should be accountable for their business decisions.

   Students should clearly state whether or not they would support forcing electric customers to pay for the power plants. Students should clearly explain the costs and benefits associated with forcing electric customers to pay for the power plants and explain why they feel their point of view is correct.

3. Students should identify the issue(s) that are involved in making it against the law for public employees to go on strike. One possible issue is the fairness of allowing private but not public employees to strike. Students should clearly state whether or not they would support a law against public employees going on strike. Students should clearly explain the costs and benefits associated with making public employee strikes illegal and explain why they feel their point of view is correct.

Problem-Solving with Economics

Chapter 3   (text pages 208–209)

1. a. An increase in taxes would reduce consumer income and *decrease* demand for all products.
   b. A baby boom would *increase* the demand for diapers by increasing the number of customers.
   c. The demand for snow shovels would *increase* at the start of December because of a change in tastes as winter started.
   d. The demand for popcorn would *increase* if the price of peanuts went up, because customers would substitute popcorn for peanuts.
   e. The demand for hospital beds would *increase* if people lived longer because there would be more old people in hospitals.
   f. The demand for all products would *increase* if people got better jobs because customers would have more income to spend.
   g. The demand for fish nets would *increase* at the start of a salmon run because of a change in tastes or possibly the number of customers.
   h. The demand for canvas shoes would

increase when leather becomes very expensive because customers would substitute canvas shoes for leather shoes they could no longer afford.

2. a. If the firm's workers are paid 10 percent more it will *increase* their costs of production and cause their supply curve to move to the *left*.
   b. If the firm has to pay more for heat it will *increase* their costs of production and cause their supply curve to move to the *left*.
   c. If the firm buys more efficient trucks it will *decrease* their costs of production and cause their supply curve to move to the *right*.
   d. If the firm installs pollution controls it will *increase* their costs of production and cause their supply curve to move to the *left*.
   e. If the firm buys a computer system it will *decrease* their costs of production and cause their supply curve to move to the *right*.
   f. If the firm spends money on training it will *decrease* their costs of production and cause their supply curve to move to the *right*.

3. a. At $5.00 30 toys would be offered for sale.
   b. At $4.00 20 toys would be offered for sale.
   c. If the price went from $3.00 to $5.00, more toys would be offered for sale.
   d. If the price went from $3.00 to $5.00, 20 more toys would be offered for sale.
   e. At $2.00 no toys would be supplied.

4. a. An increase in consumer income would cause the demand curve to move to the right and *increase* the equilibrium price.

b. A 10 percent increase in labor cost would cause the supply curve to move to the left and *increase* the equilibrium price.

c. A decrease in the cost of raw materials would cause the supply curve to move to the right and *decrease* the equilibrium price.

d. An increase in the popularity of the product would cause the demand curve to move to the right and *increase* the equilibrium price.

e. A government report that a product caused cancer would cause its demand curve to move to the left and *decrease* the equilibrium price.

f. If the raw materials become less expensive, the equilibrium price would *decrease*.

g. An increase in the price of a substitute would cause the demand curve to move to the right and *increase* the equilibrium price.

h. A decrease in exports of the product would cause the demand curve to move to the left and *decrease* the equilibrium price.

Chapter 4   (text page 209)

1. Students' lists of things they would take should include many different items. This exercise can be used to point out that no one would take more than one of any particular item. This demonstrates *diminishing marginal utility*. The first item is important but second items of the same type do not have as much value.

2. The things that students identify should be intended to shift demand, probably by affecting consumer tastes. Things like autograph sessions, or a chance to meet the players would be good ideas. Be sure to point out that giving expensive gifts

away is really little different from lowering the price of the tickets.

3. The table shows that advertisers shifted their spending from newspapers to television between 1950 and 1983. This represents a change in their demand because of a change in their tastes.

Chapter 5   (text pages 209–210)

1. The businesses identified by your students should demonstrate the following characteristics:

- The single proprietorship should be small and require relatively little capital to start. It probably will have many competitors.

- The partnership should be formed among entrepreneurs who need to share an item or service that is relatively costly. Doctors sharing the cost of a laboratory or nurse would be a good example.

- The corporation should be relatively large and require large investments in capital. The need for limited liability or professional management could also be brought out.

2. Possible fixed cost students might identify include: property taxes, mortgage payment, fire insurance, a lease on the firm's truck, weekly newspaper advertisements.

   Possible variable costs include: wages of people who set up bikes, cost of replacement parts, cost of power to run tools, cost of gas to deliver bikes, cost of ordering new bicycles.

3. There are many fixed costs associated with running a school. The costs of a library or science lab are good examples. A library costs little more to run if it has 20 or 200 students using it each day. The

costs of such facilities can be spread out among more students in large schools.

4. These firms must pay their workers whether they work or not. This means their salaries are fixed costs. It might be less expensive for these firms to produce products at a loss than to pay workers for doing nothing.

5. a. Owners of firms that want to encourage savers to invest in their business must offer a return equal to or greater than the interest banks pay. In 1977 banks paid only 5.64 percent, so businesses could attract investment by offering relatively low dividends. However, by 1981 people could deposit their savings in a bank and earn almost 16 percent interest so businesses had to pay more too.

   b. Having to pay high dividends or interest would discourage firms from making investments in new equipment.

   c. The need to pay high interest or dividends could discourage firms from renting equipment. This would cause rent paid for the use of resources to fall because of the reduced demand.

Chapter 6 (text pages 210–211)

1. a. Farms or businesses that supply basic raw materials are the best examples of pure competition. A farmer who grows corn cannot charge more than other farmers, because if he did his customers would choose to not buy his product but that of his competitors.

   b. If all firms in a competitive industry try to produce more products, the industry's total supply will increase and the equilibrium will fall.

   c. If competitive firms try to earn more money by producing and selling more products, they may force the price of their product down, causing them to earn even less income.

2. The following are possible answers:

   a. Americans buy fresh fruits and vegetables from competitive firms.

   b. Americans buy beauty products and pain relievers from firms in monopolistic competition.

   c. Americans buy automobiles and tires from firms in oligopoly.

   d. Americans buy electric power and natural gas from firms that are natural monopolies.

3. Students should demonstrate an understanding of economies and diseconomies of scale. Possible advantages (economies of scale) include (1) raw materials (cheaper when bought in quantity); (2) lower rates of interest; (3) ability to afford new machinery; (4) more efficient use of advertising.

   Possible disadvantages (diseconomies of scale) include (1) more difficult control; (2) less personal relationship with customers; (3) possibly more government controls; (4) possibly more labor problems.

4. Students should demonstrate that they have considered the costs and benefits of government ownership and have reached their decision through reason and logic.

5. a. The number of workers would increase, because each firm would need its own production, distribution, and management employees.

   b. The total cost of distribution and advertising would increase, because there would be so many firms and products to sell.

c. There would be many new soft drinks on the market.

d. The market price of soft drinks might go up if the costs of production increased enough.

e. The quantity of soft drinks sold might go down if prices increased.

Chapter 7 (text page 211)

1. a. The entry of many new, young workers into the labor force would lower wages because there would be more people competing for each job.

b. An increase in the imports of inexpensive products from other countries would lower wages because there would be fewer jobs for Americans to compete for.

c. Inflation would increase wages because fewer people would be willing to work if their wages could buy less.

d. An increase in government aid to the poor would increase wages because it would be harder for employers to attract employees who would now find it easier to not work.

2. Students should demonstrate that they have considered the merits of each of these contradictory arguments. Their decisions should be based on logic and reason.

3. Students should demonstrate that they have considered the merits of the "weapons" of labor and management. Their decisions should be based on logic and reason.

4. Two possible arguments in favor are that a lower minimum wage for young people would make it easier for them to find jobs and that a lower minimum wage for young people would give them experience.

Two possible arguments against are that a lower minimum wage for young people would result in their exploitation and that a lower minimum wage for young people would hurt older worker's chances of getting a job.

PART 3

UNDERSTANDING THE ECONOMY AS A WHOLE

CHAPTER 8

Measuring the Economy: Made in America (text pages 214–233)

SECTION A.   What is the Gross National Product? (text pages 216–220)

Objectives   (Lesson Focus)

Upon completion of this section, students will be able to:

- Define the term *Gross National Product*.
- Describe three methods used for measuring the gross national product: the expenditure approach, the income approach, and the production approach.
- Identify and explain various difficulties in measuring the gross national product accurately, including double counting and the underground economy.

Preparation   (Instruction: Pre-teaching— Vocabulary or Activity)

1. Discussion   Introduce this section by asking your students how large their yearly income would have to be to satisfy their wants and needs if they were adults with a family to support. Caution them to be reasonable and at least somewhat realistic. List these amounts on the chalkboard and figure an average for the class.

Tell your students how much the average yearly income for Americans is. It is likely that on an average your students will want a larger yearly income.

Ask your students what would happen if everyone in the country was given as much money as they would like. They should recognize that an increase in people's incomes would not increase the number of goods and services that are being produced and offered for sale. An increase in income would lead to an increase in prices. Emphasize the fact that as a group, our standard of living is limited not by the amount of money we earn but by the quantity of goods and services we produce.

2. The Personal Narrative   The Personal Narrative in Section A demonstrates our desire for more and better goods and services. The subject of the Narrative is a young woman who wants to buy a piece of new clothing. Her father feels she wants too many things. He recognizes a difference between what he provides to his daughter and what he was able to have when he was her age. He feels that there is a better use for his limited income.

The Narrative reminds students of the problem of scarcity and the fact that our demand exceeds our ability to produce goods and services. It shows that our limited GNP determines our ability to satisfy demand.

Teaching Suggestions   (Modeling/Guided Practice)

1. Ask your students what mistake was made in the following story:

   Marty repairs cars for a living. Last week he fixed the brakes on my car. He turned the disks, put on new pads, and replaced the master cylinder. When he finished he charged me $283.49. I figure he added $283.49 to the Gross National Product.

   The problem is double counting. The value of the new pads, the new master cylinder, and any other parts Marty used were added by some other firm. Only the value added by Marty's labor is part of GNP. Point out the difficulty of avoiding double counting in measuring GNP.

2. Take a survey of your students. Ask them if they earn money that they do not report to the government (outside of their own family). This could be babysitting, cutting grass, etc. This income is part of the underground economy. There are slightly over 3,000,000 high school seniors in the country. If each one earns this amount of unreported income, how much production is going unreported and untaxed (assume that all of this income would be taxed at a 15 percent rate)?

3. Explain that changes in our life-styles make it difficult to compare GNP statistics over long periods of time. For example, 50 years ago most women did not hold jobs outside of their homes. They often did work that they were not paid for, like making clothing and cleaning their house.

   Many women no longer perform these tasks but hold outside jobs instead. They buy ready-made clothes and hire services to clean their homes. Housework done by women in the past was not counted as part of GNP because it was not paid for. But work in outside jobs is compensated and is counted as part of our GNP. Why does this fact make comparisons between past and present GNP values difficult?

Lesson Checkpoint

Text: Self-Check, text page 220
   Answers

   1. The Gross National Product is the retail market value of everything produced in the nation in a year.

2. The three methods used to measure GNP are the expenditure, the income, and the production approach.

3. The underground economy represents production that is not reported to the government.

Follow-up Assignments   (Independent Practice/Extension/Homework)

Text: Applying What You Have Learned, text page 220
   Answers

   1. a. would
      b. would
      c. would not
      d. would
      e. would not
      f. would not
      g. would (it is part of his/her job)
      h. would not

   2. There is an almost unlimited number of goods that could be listed by your students. You might also discuss what their parents have that their grandparents did not have, or what they expect their children to have that they will not have.

Section Evaluation

Self-Check, text page 220
Understanding Economics, questions 1–5
   (Chapter 8 Review, text pages 230–232)

SECTION B.   What GNP Really Means (text pages 221–224)

Objectives   (Lesson Focus)

Upon completion of this section, students will be able to:

- Explain the difference between real and nominal values.
- Explain the difficulties that are experienced in attempting to equate the GNP to the quality of life.

Preparation   (Instruction: Pre-teaching—Vocabulary or Activity)

1. Discussion   Introduce this section by giving students a copy of an advertising supplement from a newspaper that is 10 or 20 years old (most libraries can help you make a copy of such an advertisement). Be sure the supplement lists many different types of items. Ask students if they feel prices were low then. Then ask what *low* means. Is a price of 40 cents for a quart of milk low if you only earn $90 a week? Point out that there are also differences in quality. A television set that was new 20 years ago is not the same as a new television today. What types of information would be necessary to talk about the standard of living 10 or 20 years ago?

2. The Personal Narrative   The Personal Narrative in Section B describes changes in a family's standard of living that resulted from their growing needs and inflation. The subject of the Narrative is a young person whose father works as a draftsman. The father has become more productive by completing special training. However, his income has not kept up with his family's needs, and inflation. Many things they could afford in the past are now too expensive.

The Narrative compares the difficulties experienced by this family with those of other people who have greater or lesser problems. It shows the difference between changes in real and nominal GNP, and how people are affected differently by these changes.

Teaching Suggestions   (Modeling/Guided Practice)

1. Use Discussion Topic 14 from the *Teacher's Resource Binder* to discuss how various products do or do not add to the quality of life.

2. Explain that although there has been an increase in real personal income in recent years, this increase has not been evenly distributed. Roughly 14 percent of the U.S. population lived in poverty in 1987. Ask your students if they would be willing to have their families pay higher taxes to support enough aid to the poor to help eliminate poverty? Why or why not?

Lesson Checkpoint

Text: Self-Check, text page 224
Answers

1. Nominal and real values differ in that real values have been adjusted for inflation but nominal values have not.

2. Real GNP *per person* includes adjustments for changes in the population.

3. The real GNP per person does not tell us the type of products that were produced, and this can have an effect on people's standards of living.

Follow-up Assignments   (Independent Practice/Extension/Homework)

Text: Applying What You Have Learned, text page 224
Answers

1. All of these are opinion answers. Many students will believe that

additional production of these items adds little to the quality of life.

2. Things that enhance the quality of life without involving money are likely to include family relationships, religion, enjoying the outdoors, and friendship.

Section Evaluation

Self-Check, text page 224
Understanding Economics, questions 6 and 7 (Chapter 8 Review, text pages 230–232)

SECTION C. Life Within the Business Cycle (text pages 225–228)

Objectives (Lesson Focus)

Upon completion of this section, students will be able to:

- Describe the four sections of the business cycle: expansion, peak, contraction, and trough.
- Identify durable and nondurable goods and explain why the sales and production of durable goods are more affected by the business cycle than nondurable goods.
- Identify and explain several leading indicators.

Preparation (Instruction: Pre-teaching— Vocabulary or Activity)

1. Discussion Introduce this section by asking your students which of the following decisions they would make if they were ten years older and believed that there was a good chance they might soon lose their jobs in a recession.

Which of the following would you decide to do?

- save more money
- buy a new car
- put off buying a swimming pool
- continue buying food
- drive your car less
- put an addition on your house
- take an expensive vacation
- buy your kids new shoes for school
- skip going to the doctor when you get sick
- register for night classes at a business college

Discuss your students' answers to these questions. How would their actions affect the economy? Would they tend to make a recession worse or not as bad? Point out that not all types of production would be affected equally. People would continue to eat even if they expected a recession.

2. The Personal Narrative The Personal Narrative in Section C describes a family that suffers from a recession. The subject of the Narrative is a young man whose father is laid off from a truck factory when sales fall during a recession. He realizes that part of the problem is caused by high truck prices and the fact that individuals and businesses are less likely to borrow money to buy expensive goods in a recession.

The Narrative demonstrates problems that result from recessions and points out that these problems are not equally distributed throughout the economy.

Teaching Suggestions (Modeling/Guided Practice)

Use Discussion Topic 15 from the *Teacher's Resource Binder* to illustrate the significance of the leading economic indicators. Read and discuss some of the better answers with your class.

Lesson Checkpoint

Text: Self-Check, text page 228
        Answers

1. The four phases of the business cycle are expansion, peak, contraction, and trough.
2. A *durable* good has a life span of several years and is likely to be expensive. *Nondurable* goods—such as food and clothing—are intended for immediate use and are likely to be less expensive.
3. Leading indicators help businesses decide whether to make additional investments.

Follow-up Assignments   (Independent Practice/Extension/Homework)

1. Text: Applying What You Have Learned, text page 228
           Answers

   a. A refrigerator is a durable good.
   b. Shampoo is a nondurable good.
   c. Gasoline is a nondurable good.
   d. Shoes are nondurable goods.
   e. A television set is a durable good.
   f. Radio batteries are nondurable goods.

2. Teacher's Resource Binder: Critical Thinking Activity, Chapter 8 (answers in Binder).

Section Evaluation

Self-Check, text page 228
Understanding Economics, questions 8 and 9 (Chapter 8 Review, text pages 230–232)

ADDITIONAL MATERIALS FOR CHAPTER 8

Chapter Evaluation

Teacher's Resource Binder: Chapter 8 Quiz

Reteaching and Extension

See the *Teacher's Resource Binder* and the *Student Activity Guide* for additional handouts and activities for Chapter 8.

TEACHER'S BIBLIOGRAPHY FOR CHAPTER 8

Economics Sources

Bowden, Elbert V. *Economics: The Science of Common Sense*, 5th ed. Cincinnati: 1986. Chapter 9 on "How to Measure National Output and Income: GNP and Price Indexes" explains the commonly used terms in national income accounting.

Gordon, Sanford D., and Dawson, George G. *Introductory Economics*, 6th ed. Lexington, Mass.: D. C. Heath, Inc., 1987. Chapter 11 provides a simple introduction to macroeconomics. Chapter 12 is a good source for the theory of income determination.

Miller, Roger LeRoy. *Economics Today*, 5th ed. New York: Harper and Row, Publishers, 1985. An excellent approach to show the various ways of compiling aggregate measurements of the economy. See Chapter 9.

Survey of Current Business. Washington, D.C.: U.S. Department of Commerce. Monthly. Contains much of the aggregate data people look for.

References for Additional Teaching Strategies

Econ/GNP (also available as Huntington I Simulation Programs). Digital Equipment

Corporation, 146 Main Street, Maynard, MA 01754. A computer-assisted game that simulates the U.S. economy. For two to ten players, playing time: 1–2 hours. Cost: $3.00.

CHAPTER 8 REVIEW ANSWERS

Building Your Vocabulary   (text page 231)

1. production approach
2. underground economy
3. nominal values
4. real values
5. leading indicator
6. income approach
7. business cycle
8. expenditure approach
9. gross national product
10. durable goods
11. nondurable goods
12. real hourly wage
13. double counting

Understanding Economics   (text page 231)

1. The new machine is part of current production (thus a part of GNP) while a used car was produced in some previous year.

2. The types of spending included in the expenditure approach to measuring GNP value are:

   a. consumption spending by individuals
   b. investment spending by businesses
   c. government spending
   d. spending by people from other countries

3. The types of earning included in the income approach to measuring GNP value are:

   a. wages
   b. profits
   c. rent
   d. interest
   e. some taxes
   f. wear out

4. Any example of double counting that shows the same contribution to GNP being counted more than once would be acceptable.

5. As more production in the underground economy goes unreported, the job of measuring the GNP becomes more difficult. This also means that those people who do not report their income pay more than their fair share to support the government in taxes.

6. A wage of $40,000 a year in 1998 means little until we know what has happened to the cost of living between the present and then.

7. An increase in real GNP could be taken up by population growth, by additional government spending, or could be distributed unequally.

8. During a recession, people and businesses are often afraid to borrow money to buy expensive durable goods. They might believe that they would not be able to repay the loan.

9. If the leading indicators have been down for five months, it would be a clear sign that the economy is going into a recession. Few people or businesses would choose to invest or grow during such a time.

Thinking Critically About Economics
(text page 232)

1. Possible answers for why GNP is not a perfect measure of the quality of life include:

   a. We would need to know about inflation.

   b. We would need to know how the GNP is distributed.

   c. We would need to know what products are being produced.

   d. We would need to know what has happened to population growth.

2. Before you could make any judgments about the $0.25 minimum wage in 1935, it would be necessary to know what goods that $0.25 could buy in that year.

3. Included in the underground economy would be:

   a. cutting your neighbor's grass and not reporting the income

   b. babysitting and not reporting the income

   c. a farmer not reporting income from a roadside stand

4. If this spending actually reduces the use of drugs in this country, it could

   a. increase spending for other goods and services

   b. reduce crime

   c. improve the productivity of people who previously used drugs

5. Car sales fell during the recession because they are expensive, durable goods. Because milk is a nondurable good, milk sales increased as the population grew.

6. a. Falling inventories show that products are being sold and will have to be replaced with new production.

   b. An increase in the hours worked reveals that workers will have more money to spend.

   c. An increase in building permits shows that there will soon be more jobs in construction.

Special Skills Projects   (text page 232)

1. Your students may need help explaining what these GNP figures show. You might consider talking about them in class before you have your students write about them.

2. Your students should find that their parents' first jobs had very different levels of pay from current entry-level jobs. When these wage rates are adjusted for inflation they will be much closer to each other. This should help your students understand the difference between real and nominal values.

3. It is possible that some of your students will come from families that underwent major economic changes because of the recession of 1981–1982. Firsthand knowledge of such events can add relevance to your discussion of the business cycle and what it means to people's lives.

CHAPTER 9

Government's Role in the Economy (text pages 234–263)

SECTION A.   Public Goods and Services (text pages 237–242)

Objectives   (Lesson Focus)

Upon completion of this section, students will be able to:

- Recognize, define, and give examples of public goods and services.

- Describe reasons for our growing need for public goods and services.
- Define and give examples of negative externalities.
- Explain the function of the government in reducing or eliminating negative externalities.
- Explain reasons for government redistribution of income.
- Explain the difference between transfer payments and transfers in kind and give examples of each.

Preparation (Instruction: Pre-teaching— Vocabulary or Activity)

1. Discussion Introduce this section by asking your students to help you make a list on the chalkboard of public goods and services from which they benefit. Help your students explain how each item on the list is paid for. Are the people who pay to support the public goods or services the same as those who benefit from them? Do your students feel there is a fair distribution of costs and benefits from the items on their list? Ask them to explain why or why not.

A second topic that could be discussed is how your students would be affected if the items on their list were not provided by the government.

2. The Personal Narrative The Personal Narrative in Section A describes public goods and services provided by the government. The subject of the Narrative is a young man who attends a public high school. The Narrative traces the events in a typical day of his life. It demonstrates how he—or his relatives and friends—benefit from public goods and services of which they may not even be aware.

The Narrative demonstrates the trade-off between the costs and benefits of public

goods and services. It also shows that these costs and benefits are not equally distributed among all people.

Teaching Suggestions (Modeling/Guided Practice)

1. Many older people do not feel that they should be expected to support public schools. They often vote against increases in school taxes when they are given an opportunity. Ask each of your students to prepare a list of ways in which older people benefit from the taxes they pay to support public schools. Combine the lists on the chalkboard and discuss them.

   How do your students feel about the prospect of paying Social Security taxes to support older retired people? Can they see any similarity between older people paying school taxes, and their own feelings regarding Social Security support?

2. Point out the fact that there are thousands of tons of radioactive waste in this country that have been produced over the years. This waste must be disposed of in one way or another. Use Discussion Topic 16 from the *Teacher's Resource Binder* to demonstrate the problem.

3. Many Americans believe that government transfers are received only by the poor. Explain that this is not the case. Virtually all Americans either currently or in the future will receive some benefit from government social programs. For example, most Americans will qualify for Social Security benefits and belong to the government's Medicare program when they retire. Children of wealthy families may be given lunches at school that are partially supported by the government. It could also be argued that stockholders in firms which received government financial assistance have in effect received a

type of transfer payment. For example, the stockholders of the Chrysler Corporation would not have done well without the government's loan guarantee in 1979.

Lesson Checkpoint

Text: Self-Check, text page 242
        Answers

    1. Unlike public goods, private goods are owned by individuals and are subject to the principle of exclusion.

    2. Continued growth and increasing specialization in the United States have increased the need for public goods and services.

    3. A negative externality occurs when someone who is neither the producer nor the consumer of a product pays a cost associated with the product.

Follow-up Assignments   (Independent Practice/Extension/Homework)

Text: Applying What You Have Learned, text page 242
        Answers

Ten public goods or services mentioned in the Personal Narrative include:

    a. a school bus

    b. sewers

    c. a traffic court

    d. police

    e. a school lunch program

    f. roads

    g. a waste treatment plant

    h. a school

    i. a traffic light

    j. a municipal arena

(There are several other acceptable answers.)

Section Evaluation

Self-Check, text page 242
Understanding Economics, questions 1 and 2 (Chapter 9 Review, text pages 260–262)

SECTION B.   Taxes and the Economy (text pages 243–247)

Objectives   (Lesson Focus)

Upon completion of this section, students will be able to:

- Identify and explain four principles of taxation: the benefits received principle, the ability-to-pay principle, the productivity principle, and the least-likely-to-offend principle.
- Define and identify examples of progressive, regressive, and proportional taxes.

Preparation   (Instruction: Pre-teaching—Vocabulary or Activity)

1. Discussion   Introduce this section by asking your class to help you list different taxes that are paid in this country. Review the types of taxes that are defined in the text on page 244. Then try to categorize each tax you have listed as an *ability-to-pay* tax, a *benefits received* tax, a *productivity* tax, or a *least-likely-to-offend* tax. The list compiled by you and your students, separated into types of taxes, should resemble the one provided below. It could be argued that several of these taxes do not clearly fall into one category only. Which taxes do your students believe are most and least fair?

Property tax is supposed to be an ability-to-pay tax but does not always work as such because property owners may not have much income. Property tax is usually regressive.

Income tax is an ability-to-pay tax; as taxable income goes up, so does the tax rate. Income tax is often progressive.

Sales tax is a least-likely-to-offend tax. It is paid in small amounts and is regressive.

Gasoline tax is a benefits received tax. Those who drive pay the tax which in turn pays for the roads. This tax is regressive.

Cigarette tax is a least-likely-to-offend tax. It is paid by smokers in small amounts and is very regressive.

Social Security tax is a benefits received tax. Those who pay by having money withheld from their paychecks throughout the years will eventually receive benefits from the program. This tax is somewhat regressive.

Tariffs are productivity taxes. By making imports more expensive, tariffs encourage people to buy American rather than foreign products. Tariffs are somewhat regressive.

Estate tax is intended to be an ability-to-pay tax. Those who inherit wealth should be able to pay the tax. Problems often occur, however, when property is inherited. Estate tax is somewhat progressive.

Corporate income tax is an ability-to-pay tax. Corporations that earn profits should be able to afford taxes. This tax is somewhat progressive.

2. The Personal Narrative The Personal Narrative in Section B demonstrates how taxes reduce our disposable income. The subject of the Narrative is a young woman who has just received her first paycheck. She is surprised by the number of ways in which her income is taxed. She feels that too much of her small income is taken by the government. She is less aware of the benefits she has

received from the government that are paid for by taxes.

The Narrative demonstrates the ways in which governments collect revenue from the people. It shows that there is a trade-off between the value a taxpayer could receive from spending income on private goods and the benefits of public goods and services that are supported through taxes.

Teaching Suggestions (Modeling/Guided Practice)

1. Ask your students to imagine they are running for a seat in their state legislature. It is clear that the state needs more money and taxes will have to be raised. There are four types of taxes listed below that could be increased. Each student should write a speech in which they identify which taxes would and would _not_ increase, and explain why. Tell them to remember they are trying to be elected.

   They could be in favor of, or opposed to, increasing: (a) state income tax by two percent, (b) state sales tax by one percent, (c) state gasoline tax by five cents a gallon, (d) state cigarette tax by twenty-five cents a pack.

2. There is almost always an argument about local taxes. Review the budgetary process of your local government with your students. List the sources of revenue. Discuss controversial issues that have resulted in tax increases. Do your students feel the increases were justified?

Lesson Checkpoint

Text: Self-Check, text page 247
       Answers

   1. The two basic principles of taxation are the _benefits received_ principle and the _ability-to-pay_ principle.

   2. In _progressive_ taxation, people with higher incomes pay a higher per-

centage of tax on their income than do people with lower incomes. In *regressive* taxation, people earning lower incomes pay a higher percentage of tax on their income than do people with higher earnings.

3. Income tax is the most important source of tax revenue for the federal government; sales tax for the state government; and property tax for local government.

Follow-up Assignments (Independent Practice/Extension/Homework)

1. Text: Applying What You Have Learned, text page 247
   Answers

   a. The $1.94 state income tax withheld from paycheck was a progressive tax.

   b. The 7 percent sales tax on the dress purchase was a regressive tax.

   c. Social Security taxes are proportional until earnings reach a limit, beyond which additional earnings are no longer taxed.

   d. The toll and parking fees were based on the benefits-received principle.

   e. The $3.56 federal withholding tax from paycheck was based on the ability-to-pay principle.

2. Ask your students to survey their adult relatives concerning taxes. Students should ask the following questions and report their findings to the class. Discuss the result of the survey in class.

   a. Roughly what part of your income do you pay in taxes?

   b. Which tax do you believe is the most reasonable?

   c. Which tax do you believe is the least reasonable?

   d. How well do you believe the government uses your tax money?

   e. What is your opinion of someone who cheats to avoid paying taxes?

Section Evaluation

Self-Check, text page 247
Understanding Economics, questions 3 and 4 (Chapter 9 Review, text pages 260–262)

SECTION C. Government Spending (text pages 248–252)

Objectives (Lesson Focus)

Upon completion of this section, students will be able to:

- Explain the difference between the decision-making process in government and in business.

- Describe the process of preparing the federal budget, including the possibility of pork-barrel legislation.

Preparation (Instruction: Pre-teaching— Vocabulary or Activity)

1. Discussion Introduce this section by asking students to review the list of public goods and services they made in Section A. Ask them to classify each item on their list as either (1) indispensable, (2) important, (3) useful, (4) of little value, or (5) a waste of money.

Combine the student lists on the chalkboard and discuss their rankings. Try to reach a consensus on what your students feel the government should and should not spend money on. Point out that it is possible to believe that the government should support a particular program without approving of the way the program is currently being run.

2. The Personal Narrative The Personal Narrative in Section C describes possible uses of and limitations on government revenues. The subject of the Narrative is a young man who lives in a southern city. He has suffered from cuts in government programs but recognizes the greater needs of other people. He is surprised by the limited number of areas in which government spending cuts can be made. He concludes that more federal aid would be one answer to local problems.

The Narrative demonstrates that government resources are limited by scarcity. It shows that a call for federal aid is a common reaction to local shortages. Many people make a distinction between money spent from local taxes and that which is supported through federal revenues.

Teaching Suggestions (Modeling/Guided Practice)

1. Ask your students to imagine that the army has been buying a particular type of weapon for the past 20 years. Each weapon costs $30,000. The government now has 15,000 of them. These weapons, however, are out-of-date, fairly inaccurate, and quite vulnerable to attack. The army would like to stop buying them. Do your students think this would be a good idea?

   Now have your students imagine they are members of the House of Representatives and that the weapon is made in their elective district. Over 2,300 people are employed making the weapon in their district, and unemployment there is already high. They must run for office again next year. Do your students think it would be a good idea for the army to stop buying the weapon under these circumstances?

   Discuss the conflict of interests demonstrated in this situation between what

is good for the nation as a whole and what is good for one local area.

2. There is almost always a "controversial" project that has been undertaken by a local government. Identify such a project for your class and discuss various points of view concerning the value of the project. Do your students feel that their tax dollars are being well spent? Is there some other type of spending they would support more?

3. Before the Social Security Act of 1935, the federal government offered little or no aid to individuals who suffered economic hardship. Today there are many programs supported with federal money that are intended to help people who are in financial difficulty.

   Some people believe that it has become too easy to be without a job in the United States. They argue that many people choose to be unemployed because they know the government will give them enough to "get by" on. Discuss this idea with your students. In their opinion, does our government do too much or too little for people who are out of work?

Lesson Checkpoint

Text: Self-Check, text page 252
Answers

1. Businesses make decisions to earn a profit; public decisions are made to directly benefit the people.

2. The preparation/writing of the federal budget is the responsibility of the president.

3. Both houses of Congress must approve the federal budget.

4. Payments to individuals is the most important type of spending performed by the federal government; educational spending is

most important for both the state and local governments.

Follow-up Assignments (Independent Practice/Extension/Homework)

Text: Applying What You Have Learned, text page 252
Answers

In the postsecondary school at the center of the photograph, students should easily recognize a number of facilities typically funded by the government (as part of a school or other public works). Most obvious are the recreational facilities: running track, tennis courts, swimming pool, baseball diamond. The postsecondary school itself is likely supported at least in part by government funds. Other items of government spending include the city streets and the traffic signals, lighting, and landscaping that accompany them. The housing tract requires sewer and water services, often a function of city government. Students may also suggest that some of the unidentified buildings may be hospitals or libraries.

Section Evaluation

Self-Check, text page 252
Understanding Economics, question 5
  (Chapter 9 Review, text pages 260–262)

SECTION D.   The Problem of the National Debt (text pages 253–258)

Objectives (Lesson Focus)
Upon completion of this section, students will be able to:

- Identify the four sources for most federal government borrowing before the 1980s: people, the banking system, businesses, and government trust funds.

- Explain that since 1980 more of this debt has been financed by sales of government securities to individuals and organizations in foreign countries.
- Describe different points of view concerning the importance of the national debt.

Preparation (Instruction: Pre-teaching—Vocabulary or Activity)

1. Discussion Introduce this section to the students by posing the following question: Which of the items below would you be willing to borrow money to obtain?

- a home
- a new car
- college tuition fees
- vacation expenses
- a new television

Point out that these items are really not all the same. Borrowing to pay for a trip to Florida is different from borrowing to go to college or to buy a car you need to get to work. Borrowing for college tuition or for a car would increase your future income; the trip to Florida would not. Ask your students what other factors they would need to consider. For example, their income and other financial responsibilities are related to the amount of money they should borrow.

Now ask students which of the following things they believe the federal government should be willing to go into debt to support:

- defense spending by the military
- more aid for colleges and universities
- environmental protection projects
- a new office building for the Senate
- rebuilding the nation's roads and waterways.

Discuss why your students would or would not support government borrowing to pay for each of these programs. Which of these programs should increase future income (production) in this country?

2. The Personal Narrative The Personal Narrative in Section D describes events that concern an individual's debt. The subject of the Narrative is a young man whose neighbor has borrowed more money than he is able to repay. The neighbor reacts to his situation by denying that the problem is his own fault. He blames both the institutions that lent him money and the people who have laid him off from his job. When he compares his borrowing to that of the federal government he sees a double standard. He does not understand why he should be in trouble for going into debt when the government borrows billions of dollars every year.

The Narrative highlights issues that concern the importance of the national debt. It asks if there is, or should be, a different set of standards for individuals and government borrowing.

Teaching Suggestions (Modeling/Guided Practice)

1. Explain that in 1987 the federal government was in debt about $10,000 for each man, woman, and child in the country. The amount of the per-person debt grew by almost $1,000 in fiscal 1985-1986 alone. The burden of this debt will be carried by future generations.

   Discuss the costs and benefits of this debt with your students. Point out that they as well as future generations will benefit in some ways from programs supported through government borrowing. Roads, canals, and buildings paid for with borrowed funds will still be here in the future for others to use. On the other hand, borrowing to support current social programs will do relatively little for future generations.

2. Discuss whether allowing foreigners to buy U.S. securities is a good idea. Some people oppose this practice because future interest payments will send money out of the country. They also feel allowing foreigners to buy our securities gives them too much influence in our economy.

   On the other hand, if we did not allow foreigners to buy our securities, our government would probably have to pay higher interest rates to borrow money. This could cause interest rates to increase, which would be bad for businesses and consumers.

   Can your students think of any other reasons why allowing foreigners to buy U.S. securities is a good or bad idea?

Lesson Checkpoint

Text: Self-Check, text page 258
      Answers

1. Until recently, four frequently used sources of government borrowing included: (a) people buying savings bonds, (b) banks and the Federal Reserve System buying bonds, (c) businesses buying bonds, and (d) government trust funds buying bonds.

2. The government has recently borrowed more money by selling securities to foreigners than it has in the past.

3. There is little consensus of opinion regarding the importance of the national debt.

Follow-up Assignments (Independent Practice/Extension/Homework)

1. Text: Applying What You Have Learned, text page 258
        Answers

(1) Two additional ways in which George's debt and the national debt differ include the following possible answers:

   a. The government can use taxation in order to obtain money to repay the national debt; George does not have this resource.

   b. George's property can be seized to satisfy his debts; such an action would not happen to the government.

(2) The seven different points of view concerning the national debt are presented on pages 255–256 of the student text. Student answers should include restatements of any four of these points of view. Look for logic and reason in the explanations for their four choices.

2. Ask your students to survey their parents about their concern for the size of the national debt. Have students ask the following questions and report their findings to the class.

   a. Do you believe the federal government should spend no more than it collects in taxes?

   b. Is there a difference between the government going into debt and an ordinary person borrowing money? If so, what is the difference.

   c. Do you believe the federal debt is too large and will cause trouble for our country in the future?

   d. Would you be willing to pay higher taxes to balance the budget?

   e. What government spending program would you cut first to help balance the budget?

3. Teacher's Resource Binder: Critical Thinking Activity, Chapter 9 (answers in Binder).

Section Evaluation

Self-Check, text page 258
Understanding Economics, question 6 (Chapter 9 Review, text pages 260–262)

ADDITIONAL MATERIALS FOR CHAPTER 9

Chapter Evaluation

Teacher's Resource Binder: Chapter 9 Quiz

Reteaching and Extension

See the *Teacher's Resource Binder* and the *Student Activity Guide* for additional handouts and activities for Chapter 9.

TEACHER'S BIBLIOGRAPHY FOR CHAPTER 9

Economics Sources

Carson, Robert B. *Economic Issues Today: Alternative Approaches.* New York: St. Martin's Press, 1987. See Issue 5, "Government Regulation of Business: Has Deregulation Worked?"

Davis, Ronnie J., and Mayer, Charles W. *Principles of Public Finance.* Englewood Cliffs, N.J.: Prentice-Hall, Inc., 1983. A good basic text. See Chapters 6 through 15.

Maxwell, James, and Aronson, Richard J. *Financing State and Local Governments.* Washington, D.C.: Brookings Institution, 1977. An excellent reference for understanding revenues and expenditures below the Federal level.

Musgrave, Richard D. and Peggy B. *Public Finance in Theory and Practice.* New York:

McGraw-Hill Book Co., 1984. A popular textbook that can be used as a reference.

Peckman, Joseph A. *Who Paid the Taxes, 1966–1985?*. Washington, D.C.: Brookings Institution, 1985. A study of the effects of federal, as contrasted with state and local, taxes and transfers of income distribution.

References for Additional Teaching Strategies

Tax Whys: Understanding Taxes. Agency for Instructional Technology, Box A, Bloomington, IN 47402. Six 15-minute video programs that help high school students to understand the principles of taxation. Programs include: "Taxes Raise Revenue," "Taxes Influence Behavior," "Taxes Involve Conflicting Goals," "Taxes Affect Different Income Goals," "Taxes . . . Can They Be Shifted?" and "Taxes . . . What is Fair?"

CHAPTER 9 REVIEW ANSWERS

Building Your Vocabulary   (text page 261)

1. principle of exclusion
2. productivity principle
3. benefits received principle
4. least-likely-to-offend principle
5. ability-to-pay principle
6. public goods
7. private goods
8. pork barrel legislation
9. progressive taxes
10. regressive taxes
11. proportional taxes
12. redistribution of income
13. negative externality
14. transfer payments; transfers in kind
15. national debt
16. intergovernmental revenues
17. social insurance tax
18. personal income tax
19. corporate income tax
20. sales tax
21. property tax

Understanding Economics   (text page 262)

1. Public goods are available to all citizens on an equal basis, while private goods are not and are subject to the principle of exclusion.

2. Examples of negative externality will probably deal with local cases of pollution.

3. The following would be acceptable examples of each of the four principles of taxation:

   a. Progressive income taxes are an ability-to-pay principle tax because the percent of income paid increases with taxable income.

   b. The gas tax is a benefits-received principle tax because the money collected is used to maintain the roads.

   c. The cigarette tax is a least-likely-to-offend principle tax because it is collected a little at a time as cigarettes are sold.

   d. Giving firms property tax cuts if they build in certain areas of many cities is an example of a productivity principle tax. If the firm invests, its taxes go down.

4. We would need to know how much money Joe and Phil earn before determining if the taxes are progressive, regressive, or proportional.

5. Decisions made by the government are often intended to help particular people or to keep a politician in office. Profit or economic efficiency often has little to do

with these decisions. In business, decisions are made to increase profits and are based on achieving economic efficiency.

6. Before 1980, the four most important sources of borrowed money for the federal government were:

   a. people who bought savings bonds

   b. banks and other financial institutions

   c. businesses

   d. government trust funds

   After 1980, foreign sources of borrowing became more important to the U.S. government.

Thinking Critically About Economics
(text page 262)

1. Most public goods mentioned by students could not be purchased by most individuals. Most of your students would have to do without these things if they were not provided by the government.

2. By requiring pollution control devices on cars the government forced car prices up but reduced the danger to the public health that had been posed by automobile pollution. The cost was paid by the customer and the producer instead of by third parties that had nothing to do with the production or use of the cars.

3. Answers to be based on graphs in Figures 9-2 and 9-3 in text:

   a. Federal—personal income tax; State—sales tax; Local—property tax

   b. Federal—payments to individuals; State—education; Local—education

4. A cut in taxes will not help just one part of the country and therefore just one politician. A new port would be in just one location and could therefore help one particular politician.

5. If the debt is held by foreign people, future interest payments will send money out of this country.

6. Between 1945 and 1980, the national debt fell as a percent of GNP. After 1980 the national debt increased as a percent of GNP.

Special Skills Projects   (text page 262)

1. Your students will probably find different opinions of transfer payments among the people who receive them. People who are dependent on such payments will probably think they are far too small. People who have other sources of income or who have saved will probably think they are large enough, or at least not be as upset about them.

2. You may want to spend adequate time comparing how your local government spends its money and how other local governments spend theirs. Urban and suburban areas are often quite different in the way they spend money.

CHAPTER 10

Inflation, Unemployment, and the Distribution of Income (text pages 264–287)

SECTION A.   The Costs of Unemployment (text pages 267–270)

Objectives   (Lesson Focus)

Upon completion of this section, students will be able to:

- Define, identify examples of, and explain frictional, seasonal, cyclical, and structural unemployment.

- Explain the meaning of the term *discouraged worker*.

Preparation (Instruction: Pre-teaching—Vocabulary or Activity)

1. Discussion Introduce this section by identifying the largest single employer in the area of your school. Ask your students to describe what would happen in your community if this firm closed down. People who had worked for the firm would be affected first but soon others would be too. Former employees would not be able to spend as much money, so local businesses and their employees would suffer. Banks would be hurt if people could not pay back loans. The local government would collect less money in sales taxes and might have to lay off some workers. Make the point that unemployment would strike those who worked for the firm first but that its effects would eventually spread to the entire community.

2. The Personal Narrative The Personal Narrative in Section A is a conversation between people who are waiting in line to receive unemployment compensation checks. Each of the subjects of the Narrative is unemployed for a different reason and demonstrates a different type of unemployment.

The Narrative demonstrates four basic types of unemployment and describes problems associated with each. It shows different reasons for unemployment and demonstrates how unemployment affects people in different ways.

Teaching Suggestions (Modeling/Guided Practice)

1. Ask each student to identify the specific job they would like to hold in ten years. Then have them explain, either orally or in writing, how they believe this job would or would not be affected by a future recession in the economy. You may want to use their answers to lead into a discussion of career choice.

2. Invite a person who does hiring for a local firm to come to talk to your class. Ask this person to talk about what they look for when they are interviewing a potential employee. You could also ask the speaker to discuss possible causes for a current employee to be fired. Use this information to start a discussion of how students can prepare themselves to find the job they want.

Lesson Checkpoint

Text: Self-Check, text page 270
Answers

1. Because of frictional unemployment—people moving within the work force—there will always be at least 4 to 5 percent unemployment.

2. Structural unemployment is considered to be the most serious type because to remedy it requires training, which is a long and costly process for both the individual and the economy as a whole.

3. The government classifies discouraged workers as those who have given up in their search for employment.

Follow-up Assignments (Independent Practice/Extension/Homework)

1. Text: Applying What You Have Learned, text page 270
Answers

(1) a. Jerry represented structural unemployment.

b. Tina represented frictional unemployment.

c. Shawn represented seasonal unemployment.

d. James represented cyclical unemployment.

(2) Students could (a) develop good math and reading skills, which would help them move from one type of job to another if it became necessary, (b) broaden their knowledge to include many different things that would help them in the labor market, and (c) train for jobs that will always be necessary, such as in the health care industry.

2. Almost all students know an adult who has changed jobs, either through choice or necessity. Assign your students to interview at least one such adult. Have them ask the following questions and report their findings to the class:

a. What was your previous job and why did you leave it?

b. What is your current job and how long did it take you to find it?

c. Do you believe your new job is better or worse than your old job? Why do you believe this?

d. Did you suffer any economic hardship when you changed jobs? If so, describe the hardship.

e. Did you need any special training to qualify for your new job that you did not need for your previous job?

   Help your students identify the type of unemployment involved in each job change reported. Were all people affected in the same ways by their job change?

3. Teacher's Resource Binder: Critical Thinking Activity, Chapter 10 (answers in Binder).

Section Evaluation

Self-Check, text page 270
Understanding Economics, questions 1 and 2
   (Chapter 10 Review, text pages 284–286)

SECTION B.   Life with Inflation (text pages 271–276)

Objectives   (Lesson Focus)

Upon completion of this section, students will be able to:

- Explain how the consumer price index is determined and used.
- Explain the difference between demand-pull inflation and cost-push inflation and recognize examples of each.
- Describe the effects of inflation and explain why it does not affect all people equally.

Preparation   (Instruction: Pre-teaching—Vocabulary or Activity)

1. Discussion   Introduce this section by asking each student to list five items they frequently buy. Ask them to explain what they would do if the price of these items doubled. Point out that although prices have not recently doubled in the United States, they did increase over slightly 100 percent between 1971 and 1980. Discuss different ways in which people react to higher prices. They can

a. decide not to buy as many items.

b. buy the same items and save less for the future.

c. demand higher wages or profits.

d. buy lower quality, less expensive goods instead.

e. take a second job to earn more money.

   Point out that not all people are equally able to do these things. A person who is retired and lives on a fixed income is not in a position to demand higher wages. He or she may also be too sick or weak to take a job and thus may be forced to do without needed goods or services. A person who is young, healthy, and holds a good job is less likely to be harmed by inflation.

2. The Personal Narrative The Personal Narrative in Section B describes how people are affected by inflation. The subjects of the Narrative are several young men who have gone to a movie where they find the price of admission has been increased. This forces them to choose between either paying the higher price and giving up other things they would have liked to buy or not going to the movie.

The Narrative discusses several possible causes of inflation and different ways in which people react to it. The Narrative also shows that people are not equally affected by inflation.

Teaching Suggestions (Modeling/Guided Practice)

1. Tell your students to imagine that they have asked one of their parents for ten dollars to help pay for a date. Instead of the money, they receive a speech about their parent's first job in 1962, which only paid $.90 an hour. Assign them to write an essay in which they logically explain why the amount that could be earned in 1962 has little to do with the present.

2. Explain that one of the most important causes of inflation is the *expectation* of inflation. Ask your students to describe what they would do in each of the following situations if they honestly believed prices would increase 12 percent next year.

   a. They are negotiating for a wage increase for next year.
   b. They are deciding what price to charge for their product.
   c. They are deciding how much interest they will accept from someone who wants to borrow money from them.

   d. They are deciding how much more they want for a piece of property they have decided to sell.
   e. They are considering whether or not to take a job that pays the minimum wage.

   Point out that in each of these cases the expectation of inflation will encourage people to make decisions that will tend to cause inflation. The expectation of inflation is a self-fulfilling prophecy. If we all believe there will be inflation, it will probably take place.

3. Not all items are affected equally by inflation. The value of some items tends to increase with an increase in prices, while the value of other items does not. Explain that many people try to "hedge" against inflation by investing in different ways. Ask your students which of the following they would rather have if prices were increasing at 12 percent:

   a. $10,000 in cash
   b. $10,000 deposited in a bank that pays 8 percent interest
   c. $10,000 invested in the stock of a utility that pays a 10 percent dividend
   d. $10,000 invested in land near a place where the state is thinking of building an important highway
   e. $10,000 invested in gold and silver coins

   Point out that the possibility of a higher return is associated with greater amounts of risk. Investing in gold coins may have a high potential for return, but it also has substantial risk. There is the possibility that the price of gold will go down or that its increase in value will not keep up with inflation. People who have no money to invest, of course, are not in a position to hedge against inflation and may be hurt the most.

Lesson Checkpoint

Text: Self-Check, text page 276
        Answers

1. The CPI (Consumer Price Index) is found through a survey of several hundred goods and services. The prices for the goods and services are totaled and compared with their levels at the base year.

2. Cost-push inflation is associated with a movement of the supply curve to the left.

3. Demand-pull inflation is associated with a movement of the demand curve to the right.

Follow-up Assignments   (Independent Practice/Extension/Homework)

Text: Applying What You Have Learned, text page 276
        Answer

In the situation presented in the Personal Narrative, increases in the rental price of the property where the theater was located and in the wages paid to theater employees contributed to increases in theater ticket and concession prices.

Section Evaluation

Self-Check, text page 276
Understanding Economics, questions 3–6
   (Chapter 10 Review, text pages 284–286)

SECTION C.   The Distribution of Wealth and Income (text pages 277–282)

Objectives   (Lesson Focus)

Upon completion of this section, students will be able to:

■ Explain why poverty is not the same in all countries.

■ Explain the difference between income and wealth.

■ Read a Lorenz Curve.

Preparation   (Instruction: Pre-teaching—Vocabulary or Activity)

1. Discussion   Introduce this section by asking your students how much income they would have to earn to feel that they were rich. Remind them that it is not really the income that they care about but what the income will buy. As long as we can produce a limited supply of goods and services, there can only be a limited number of rich people.

Ask them what characteristics of a person's standard of living would indicate that he was poor. Is poverty not having a place to live and food to eat, or is it not owning a car or a new television set? Does poverty have anything to do with how people feel about themselves? Could a person live in a log cabin in a forest, eating only what he grew and gathered for himself, and not be poor?

Try to help your students reach a consensus about what makes a person rich or poor. Ask them to what degree they feel society has a responsibility to aid poor people.

2. The Personal Narrative   The Personal Narrative in Section C describes how one person is aware of differences in the distribution of income and wealth. The subject of the Narrative is a young man who sees a world in which some people are very wealthy while others are in need. He does not understand why there is such inequity in a country that has so much wealth.

The Narrative points out problems that are related to the unequal distribution of income and wealth in the United States. It concludes with a common assumption that giving poor people more income would solve their problems. The remainder of the section will show that this is not necessarily a correct assumption.

Teaching Suggestions   (Modeling/Guided Practice)

Explain that there is disagreement among government leaders over whether new technology will reduce or increase poverty. Some people say new machines will produce more goods which will allow more people to have a better standard of living. Others argue that new machines will take low-skill jobs from poor people while they earn greater profits for the wealthy. They believe that new technology will make the difference between the rich and the poor even larger than it is now.

Discuss this question with your students: What will new technology do to the distribution of income and wealth? Point out that to remain competitive in the world economy, the United States is almost compelled to invest in new technology. Can we afford to be inefficient in order to protect jobs for some people?

Lesson Checkpoint

Text: Self-Check, text page 282
Answers

1. The federal government's definition of poverty is based on studies that provide an estimate of what is necessary to supply an adequate diet for a family of four living in a city.

2. Income is a flow of value; wealth is an accumulation of value.

3. A Lorenz Curve is used to show the distribution of income.

Follow-up Assignments   (Independent Practice/Extension/Homework)

1. Text: Applying What You Have Learned, text page 282
Answers

Although there are many possible answers, students should recognize that people who live in pov-erty have many problems beyond a lack of money. Many poor people would not know how to use sudden, large amounts of money to make permanent improvements in their standard of living. They might waste it or someone who was dishonest might take it from them. Money would not give them skills or good jobs.

2. Have each of your students survey five adults and report their findings to the class. They should ask each adult the following questions:

   a. What does poverty mean in the United States?

   b. Do you feel there are more or less poor people in this country now than there were five years ago?

   c. What reasons can you give for any change in the number of poor people over the past five years?

   d. Do you expect the number of poor people to increase or decrease over the next five years?

   e. Would you be willing to pay higher taxes so the government could give more aid to poor people?

Section Evaluation

Self-Check, text page 282
Understanding Economics, questions 7 and 8 (Chapter 10 Review, text pages 284–286)

ADDITIONAL MATERIALS FOR CHAPTER 10

Chapter Evaluation

Teacher's Resource Binder: Chapter 10 Quiz

Reteaching and Extension

See the *Teacher's Resource Binder* and the *Student Activity Guide* for additional handouts and activities for Chapter 10.

TEACHER'S BIBLIOGRAPHY FOR CHAPTER 10

Economics Sources

Gowland, David. *Money, Employment and Inflation.* New York: Barnes and Noble Imports, 1985. Shows how inflation and the money supply are related and how the employment rate influences the inflationary rate. Short and simple.

McLeod, Alex. *The Fearsome Dilemma: Simultaneous Inflation and Unemployment.* Lanham, Md.: University Press of America, 1985. A relatively short work on stagflation that is suitable for both students and teachers.

A Primer on Inflation. The Federal Reserve Bank of New York, 33 Liberty Street, New York, NY 10045, 1984. A 16-page pamphlet that defines inflation, discusses its causes, and suggests how to deal with it.

You and Your Money. The Federal Reserve Bank of Richmond, P.O. Box 27622, Richmond, VA 23261, 1981. A 14-page pamphlet that discusses the causes and suggested remedies for inflation.

References for Additional Teaching Strategies

Inflation . . . Taxing the American Dream. Federal Reserve Bank of New York, 33 Liberty Street, New York, NY 10045, 1980. Materials include two filmstrips with cassettes, the comic book-styled "The Story of Inflation," three reproducible activity masters, and a teacher's manual.

Morton, John S., et al. *High School Economics Courses.* New York: Joint Council on Economic Education, 2 Park Avenue, New York, NY 10016, 1985. See Lessons 16 and 17.

Inflation in the Eighties. Social Studies School Service, P.O. Box 802, Culver City, CA 90230, price $30. Two color filmstrips with cassettes and teaching guide. The first deals with different types of inflation and the effects of government actions. The second is oriented around the individual and how to cope with inflation.

CHAPTER 10 REVIEW ANSWERS

Building Your Vocabulary   (text page 285)

1. inflation
2. consumer price index
3. cost-push inflation
4. demand-pull inflation
5. income; wealth
6. base year
7. frictional unemployment
8. structural unemployment
9. cyclical unemployment
10. discouraged workers
11. seasonal unemployment
12. Lorenz Curve
13. poverty

Understanding Economics   (text page 285)

1. Student examples should be:

   a. someone who is unemployed short term and is between jobs

   b. someone who loses employment during a particular time of each year

   c. someone who has lost employment due to a recession

   d. someone who has lost employment and will require retraining

2. A person who is designated as unemployed by the government is actively looking for work while a discouraged worker has given up trying to find work.

3. Factors that could cause the supply curve to shift to the left include an increase in

the cost of labor or of raw materials. This would cause cost-push inflation.

4. Factors that could cause the demand curve to shift to the right include an increase in consumer income or an increase in government spending. This would cause demand-pull inflation.

5. The consumer price index is found by surveying several hundred items in several thousand outlets each month. Some items are counted more often than others because consumers buy them more often. The total for each month is compared to the total from some base time. Changes are expressed as percentage changes of this base time.

6. People that lend money can be hurt by inflation if it makes the purchasing power of the money they are paid back less than the money they lent out.

7. Poverty is measured in relation to what other people in the communities have. Most poor people in the United States are not starving and most have a place to live. In many other countries this is not the case. In many parts of Africa, for example, poverty means starvation.

8. Income is a flow of value while wealth is an accumulation of value.

Thinking Critically About Economics
(text page 286)

1. Structural unemployment is the worse type of unemployment for both the economy and the individual because it requires retraining. This is a long expensive process. During this retraining period, the worker will add little value to production or to the support of his or her family.

2. Possible reasons for becoming a discouraged worker include:

a. lack of an adequate education
b. lack of job experience
c. lack of success in job hunting
d. poor health
e. old age

3. Possible reasons for the different rates of employment include:

a. discrimination in hiring
b. different quality of education available to different groups
c. different socioeconomic backgrounds

4. The increase in the price of crude oil caused cost-push inflation because crude oil is a basic raw material for many types of products. This increase in the cost of production was passed on to customers in the form of higher prices.

5. Four possible answers illustrating how inflation hurts people are:

a. reducing the value of their savings
b. reducing their ability to buy goods and services
c. forcing interest rates up
d. making it harder to sell products to other countries

6. If everyone had the same standard of living, there would be little reason to work hard to produce goods and services. The number of products manufactured would probably fall.

7. Student answers should make it clear that they understand poverty is defined in terms of community standards and not by absolutes.

Special Skills Projects   (text page 286)

1. Your students will probably find that people who have been unemployed for an extended period of time have a differ-

ent outlook on life than people who have never experienced such economic hardship. Some may react by becoming very cautious; others may have a more "live-for-today" attitude.

2. Your students will probably find that the prices of some items have changed very little over the past ten years, while others have increased a great deal. Help them to understand why there has not been uniform inflation. What does this tell them about the relative demand and supply for these different items?

3. It may be hard to measure changes, but there should be a small trend to a less equal distribution of income. If this trend can be found, discuss what causes there may have been for the change and what it shows about changes in the U.S. society as well as the economy.

Chapter 11

Money and the Economy (text pages 288–317)

SECTION A. What Money Is and Where It Came From (text pages 291–296)

Objectives (Lesson Focus)

Upon completion of this section, students will be able to:

- Explain what money is in economic terms.
- Identify the functions and characteristics of money.
- Explain the relationship between changes in the money supply, changes in the quantity of products offered for sale, and changes in price levels.

Preparation (Instruction: Pre-teaching—Vocabulary or Activity)

1. Discussion Introduce this section by describing a society in which there is no money. All transactions are made through barter. Ask your students to explain why each of the following transactions would be difficult in such a society. Identify the function or characteristic of money demonstrated in each situation.

a. You own a cow that you want to trade for a pig and a new tent. The pig belongs to one person, while someone else owns the tent you want. (*money must be divisible*)

b. You want to trade some chickens for a new cooking pot. The person who makes cooking pots does not want any chickens. (*money must be accepted*)

c. You want to save up for a new house. You grow fresh fruit for a living. (*money is a store of value*)

d. You want to trade your goat for eight chickens, but the owner of the chickens will only give you six of them in exchange for your goat. (*money is a measure of value*)

e. You make stone corn grinders for a living. You have to pay a large debt to someone who lives 50 miles away. (*money must be portable*)

Discuss the fact that all advanced economic systems require a form of money that possesses the characteristics listed in the text, so that it can perform the functions of money in the economy.

2. The Personal Narrative The Personal Narrative in Section A illustrates that something which has value does not necessarily have to be money. The subject of the Narrative is a young man who has inherited a gold watch from his grandfather. He recognizes that the watch has value but that it would be difficult to use its value to buy anything else without first selling the watch. The watch is not money for many reasons, which include the fact that people do not agree on the amount of value it has and that its value is not divisible.

Teaching Suggestions (Modeling/Guided Practice)

1. Ask students how they would feel if an uncle had left them $1 million. They would probably be happy about the money although they might not be happy with the death of their uncle. Ask them to identify several items they would buy with the money.

   Extend the example by telling the students that the uncle was very rich and left everyone in the United States a million dollars. How much better off would the students be if everyone had the same amount of additional money? Would they be able to buy the items they identified above?

   Simply because people had more money to spend would not provide additional products available to buy. The extra money would force prices up. Each individual would end up being able to buy about the same amount of goods and services as they could before. Remind your students that money is not important: it is what you can buy with money that people care about. Discuss how this example relates to Figure 11-1 in the text.

2. Use Discussion Topic 17 from the *Teacher's Resource Binder* to reinforce the nature of money and the significance of the money supply.

Lesson Checkpoint

Text: Self-Check, text page 296
   Answers

   1. Economists define *money* as a claim on something that possesses value; in other words, money represents value but rarely has any intrinsic value of its own.

   2. The three functions of money identified in this section included: money as a medium of exchange, as a measure of value, and as a store of value.

   3. When the availability of money grows more rapidly than the amount of goods and services offered for sale, prices go up and inflation exists.

Follow-up Assignments (Independent Practice/Extension/Homework)

1. Text: Applying What You Have Learned, text page 296
   Answers

   Possible problems the young man could have encountered in trying to use his watch as money include:

   a. The watch lacked a clear definition of value.

   b. The watch would not have been universally accepted.

   c. The value of the watch was not easily divisible.

   d. There was no way to determine if the value of the watch would remain the same in the future.

2. Some adults do not understand the relationship between prices and the amount of money in circulation. Ask students to

survey five adults who do not work at their school. They should ask this single question: "What would happen if the government simply printed the money it needs to pay its bills?" Have students individually report the results of their surveys to the class as a whole. What percentage of adults surveyed realized such a policy would cause inflation?

Section Evaluation

Self-Check, text page 296
Understanding Economics, questions 1 and 2 (Chapter 11 Review, text pages 314–316)

SECTION B. Checks, Money, and the Economy (text pages 297–301)

Objectives (Lesson Focus)

Upon completion of this section, students will be able to:

- Follow the flow of a check through the economy using the chart provided in this text.
- Explain what the term "reserve requirement" means.
- Explain how money can be expanded through checking accounts by the banking system.
- Recognize the meaning, and explain the use of, the expansion multiplier.

Preparation (Instruction: Pre-teaching—Vocabulary or Activity)

1. Discussion Introduce this section by asking students to list three of the most important financial transactions they ever expect to make. They will probably identify such transactions as buying a house or a car, paying college tuition, starting a business, or paying for an expensive vacation.

Consolidate the individual lists on the chalkboard. Ask your students if there are any transactions on the list that they would expect to make in cash. Point out the fact that almost all large transactions are carried out with demand deposits or checks. This means that the government must control the checking system if it wants to control spending in the economy.

2. The Personal Narrative The Personal Narrative in Section B describes how one family uses demand deposits to pay its bills and how the checking system is part of the money supply in our economy. The subject of the Narrative is a young woman whose father uses checks to pay the family's bills. She describes how she came to understand how checks work when she got a job. She also realizes that if the government wants to control the money supply, it must first control the checking system.

The Narrative demonstrates how checks are used in our economic system and why they are such an important part of our money supply.

Teaching Suggestions (Modeling/Guided Practice)

1. Ask your students to sit in a large circle. Hand one student 200 fake one dollar bills and a numbered sheet of paper for tabulation. (The money must be entirely in ones; using larger bills for this exercise would be confusing.) Tell the first student to write $200 on the paper after number 1. Then tell the student to keep twenty of the dollars and to pass the remaining $180 and the tabulation paper to the next student. This student writes $180 on the sheet, keeps $18, and passes the remaining money and the tabulation paper on to the next student. The pro-

cess is repeated until all students have done it, keeping 10 percent of the money (rounded to the nearest full dollar) and passing on the rest. When all students have completed the process, total the amounts on the tabulation paper.

Explain how this exercise is similar to the expansion of an original $200 deposit through the banking system when there is a 10 percent reserve requirement. Each time money is passed from one student to another, they are to assume that a bank has made a loan, the money has been spent, and redeposited into the banking system. Each successive student represents another bank that must keep 10 percent of the deposit on reserve. The remaining 90 percent can be loaned out as the next step in the process.

The table below indicates how much each student should pass on.

Student/Amount	Student/Amount
1/$180	16/$37
2/$162	17/$33
3/$146	18/$30
4/$131	19/$27
5/$118	20/$24
6/$106	21/$22
7/$ 96	22/$20
8/$ 86	23/$18
9/$ 77	24/$16
10/$ 70	25/$14
11/$ 63	26/$13
12/$ 56	27/$12
13/$ 51	28/$10
14/$ 46	29/$ 9
15/$ 41	30/$ 8

2. Repeat the same process as above, but this time use a reserve requirement of 12 percent. Note the difference in the expansion of the original $200. Again, the amounts in the table below have been rounded to the nearest full dollar, and are what should be passed on.

Student/Amount	Student/Amount
1/$176	16/$26
2/$155	17/$23
3/$136	18/$20
4/$120	19/$18
5/$106	20/$16
6/$ 93	21/$14
7/$ 82	22/$12
8/$ 72	23/$11
9/$ 63	24/$ 9
10/$ 56	25/$ 8
11/$ 49	26/$ 7
12/$ 43	27/$ 6
13/$ 38	28/$ 6
14/$ 33	29/$ 5
15/$ 29	30/$ 4

Compare the total expansion with the two differing reserve requirements of 12 percent and 10 percent. Point out how powerful a change in the reserve requirement would be when the entire economy is considered. A one-percent change in the reserve requirement would change the money supply by many billions of dollars.

Lesson Checkpoint

Text: Self-Check, text page 301
Answers

1. Over 80 percent of all spending is done with checks.

2. The reserve requirement is the percentage of the deposit that the law says a bank must keep on reserve.

3. Banks normally keep more money in reserve than is required, and people hold onto cash rather than depositing it in banks.

Follow-up Assignments (Independent Practice/Extension/Homework)

1. Text: Applying What You Have Learned, text page 301
Answers

Advantages of checks include:

a. They are safer to use than cash.

b. They are easier to carry than large amounts of cash.

c. They provide a record of transactions.

d. They can only be used by the person to whom they are written.

2. Ask your students to survey their parents concerning what part of their total spending is done with checks. Students should also ask their parents to identify the types of payments they make with checks. Have the students report their findings to the class. Students should discover that many adults do most of their spending with checks. Are there any generalizations that can be made about the kind of spending carried out with checks?

Section Evaluation

Self-Check, text page 301
Understanding Economics, questions 3–5 (Chapter 11 Review, text pages 314–316)

SECTION C. Banks Are in Business to Make a Profit (text pages 302–305)

Objectives (Lesson Focus)

Upon completion of this section, students will be able to:

- Explain why banks would follow procyclical policies if they were allowed to by the Federal Reserve System.
- Explain the function and importance of the Federal Deposit Insurance Corporation.
- Identify typical bank assets and liabilities.

Preparation (Instruction: Pre-teaching—Vocabulary or Activity)

1. Discussion Introduce this section by asking each student to think of their best friend. Then tell them to imagine that this person asked to borrow $500 (they should also imagine they had the money to lend if they wanted to). Ask your students to make a list of reasons that might cause them to make the loan. Also ask them to make a second list of reasons that could cause them to deny the loan. Ask them which of their reasons would be important to a bank and which would not. Point out that although friendship may be an important reason for them, it would have little to do with the decision of a bank. Remind them that banks are businesses that intend to make a profit.

2. The Personal Narrative The Personal Narrative in Section C describes how an individual business can be hurt by a downturn in the local economy and how these problems can be aggravated by the actions of banks. The subject of the Narrative is a young man whose father works as a gardener. When there is a water shortage, many of his customers are not allowed to use his services. Because his business is not doing well, his bank is unwilling to loan him the money he needs.

The Narrative demonstrates that banks are in business to make a profit. The decisions they make are based on economic conditions and their perception of risk. Banks will not loan money unless they believe it will be repaid.

Teaching Suggestions (Modeling/Guided Practice)

1. Invite a loan officer from a bank to talk to your students. The topic of the interview should be the importance of a good

credit rating and how a young person can establish such a credit rating. (If you can't find a loan officer who is willing to meet with your class, it may be possible to find one who will agree to be interviewed by a student.) Whether you send a student to interview a loan officer or have one visit your class, take the time to prepare good questions. You do not want your guest to think the interview is a waste of time. A list of possible questions appears below:

a. What are the advantages of having a good credit rating?

b. What can a young person do to develop a good credit rating?

c. If a bank turns you down when you ask for a loan, what rights do you have?

d. If a person feels he or she has been unjustly denied credit, what can he or she do?

e. How does a bank decide how much money it is willing to loan to a person or to a business?

f. If a person fails to make payments on a loan, what actions will a bank take?

g. Why are there different interest rates for different types of loans?

h. What is the effect of getting married or divorced on a person's credit rating?

2. The following list of items often appears on a bank's balance sheet. Help your class determine where each item would appear on the bank's balance sheet. Determine which items would appear on the left side with assets or on the right side with liabilities.

a. a one year certificate of deposit (right side)

b. a car loan it has made (left side)

c. a deposit in a checking account (right side)

d. a loan it has received from another bank (right side)

e. cash (left side)

f. its office building (left side)

g. a loan it has made to another bank (left side)

h. its stockholder's equity (right side)

i. money it has borrowed from the Federal Reserve System (right side)

j. government securities it has purchased (left side)

3. Emphasize the importance of the Federal Deposit Insurance Corporation. Ask your students if they would be willing to deposit their savings in a bank that did not belong to the FDIC. Remind them that prior to 1935 there was no FDIC; if banks failed, depositors often lost part or all of their savings. Help your students appreciate the fact that without the FDIC our banking system could not work as well as it does. Many people would not deposit their money into banks. This would reduce the effectiveness of the expansion of money.

Lesson Checkpoint

Text: Self-Check, text page 305
Answers

1. Banks earn a profit by charging their borrowers a higher interest rate than they pay their depositors.

2. *Pro-cyclical* refers to policies that would increase any existing economic trends.

3. The FDIC insures deposits in order to maintain public confidence in banks.

Follow-up Assignments (Independent Practice/Extension/Homework)

1. Text: Applying What You Have Learned, text page 305
   Answers

   Students will likely include the following three factors to explain why the bank considered the man in the Personal Narrative to be a poor credit risk for a loan.

   a. His debts and other obligations exceeded his financial capacity to repay them in a timely manner.
   b. His cyclical employment as a gardener created an unstable demand for his services; therefore, his employment record was insecure.
   c. He had few assets to pledge as collateral for a loan, and little equity had been built up in his residence.

2. Teacher's Resource Binder: Critical Thinking Activity, Chapter 11 (answers in Binder).

Section Evaluation

Self-Check, text page 305
Understanding Economics, questions 6 and 7 (Chapter 11 Review, text pages 314–316)

SECTION D.   What the Federal Reserve System Does (text pages 306–311)

Objectives (Lesson Focus)

Upon completion of this section, students will be able to:

- Describe the conditions that resulted in the creation of the Federal Reserve System.

- Define monetary policy and explain the basic tools of monetary policy used by the Federal Reserve System: adjusting the reserve requirement, discount rate, and open market operation.
- Describe several examples of uses the Federal Reserve has made of its monetary powers.

Preparation (Instruction: Pre-teaching—Vocabulary or Activity)

1. Discussion Introduce this section by asking students to pretend they are in business and are considering five potential investments. Remind them that they are in business to make a profit. They would only borrow money if they expected to earn more than the cost of the loan. Their firm would have to borrow money to pay for any of the projects they are considering. The table below indicates the expected rate of return (profit) from each possible investment.

Investment	Expected Return	Cost
1. a new truck to make quicker deliveries	8.1%	$ 20,000
2. a new machine for the assembly line	10.1%	$ 70,000
3. a new computer to control inventory	12.1%	$ 50,000
4. an expansion of the factory	9.1%	$250,000
5. insulation to reduce heating costs	11.1%	$ 80,000

Help your students figure out how much money the firm would borrow at each of the possible interest rates listed below (answers are provided in the second column):

Interest Rate	Amount Borrowed
8%	$470,000
9%	$450,000
10%	$200,000
11%	$130,000
12%	$50,000
13%	$0

Use this exercise to show your students how important interest rates are to business spending and therefore to employment and earnings in the economy as a whole.

2. The Personal Narrative The Personal Narrative in Section D demonstrates the importance of Federal Reserve policies to the economy. The subject of the Narrative is a young man whose father is an architect. The family's income is sensitive to changes in interest rates. When interest rates grow, there is often less construction and consequently less work for his father. When interest rates fall, there is often more contruction and work for his father. The young man realizes that interest rates are affected by decisions made by the Federal Reserve System. He sees that there is a relationship between his father's success and the actions of the Federal Reserve System, but he doesn't understand how the relationship works.

The Narrative shows students that decisions made by the Federal Reserve System are important both to the economy as a whole and to each individual.

Teaching Suggestions (Modeling/Guided Practice)

1. Ask your students to pretend they have all become members of the Federal Reserve's Board of Governors. They have agreed that too many loans are being made. Businesses are spending far too much money and are trying to hire more workers than there are people looking for work. People are also borrowing and spending large amounts of money. Although the situation is not yet totally out of control, the rate of inflation is clearly increasing. There have been three suggestions made on what should be done. Ask your students which of the following suggestions should or should not be put

into action. Help them explain and evaluate each suggestion, either in writing or orally.

Suggestion 1: Increase the reserve requirement on demand deposits from 12 percent to 14 percent.

Suggestion 2: Increase the discount rate from 7 percent to 7½ percent.

Suggestion 3: Sell $1 billion worth of government securities.

2. Divide your students into groups of three to five students. For each describe one of the following situations. Ask each group to either (a) agree on the best policy for the Federal Reserve to follow in their situation *or* (b) explain why a policy change by the Fed would not solve the problem. If you feel that these situations are too challenging for your students, you could choose to discuss them together in class. (For your reference, the desired student responses to each individual situation are included here as well. Suggested responses are italicized and parenthesized directly following each respective situation.)

Situation 1
The economy is in a very deep depression. Individuals and businesses seem afraid to borrow money no matter what the interest rates are. (*If individuals and businesses are really afraid to borrow money, there may be little the Fed can do to get the economy moving. People could simply ignore extra money that was put into circulation.*)

Situation 2
The economy has had a high rate of inflation over the past year, largely be-

cause the cost of imported goods and raw materials has increased by over 35 percent. *(If the inflation is caused by increased prices for imports, there is probably little the Fed can do to solve the problem. People in other countries who sell to the United States often do not care what interest rates are in this country.)*

Situation 3

There has been a large decline in new housing construction because people who want to buy homes have found it difficult to borrow money or don't want to pay high interest rates. *The Fed would probably buy government securities to increase the money in circulation and to reduce interest rates. It would be less likely to lower the discount rate or the reserve requirement.)*

Situation 4

Interest rates are a little lower than the Fed would like them to be for all types of loans. *(The Fed would probably sell a few government securities to decrease the money in circulation and to increase interest rates. It would be less likely to increase the discount rate or the reserve requirement.)*

Situation 5

The treasury has been borrowing large amounts of money by selling government securities. This has resulted in a temporary shortage of money for banks to loan to other people and in higher interest rates. *(The Fed might ignore what the treasury is doing or it could choose to buy more government securities to supply more money and keep interest rates down. This policy could lead to higher rates of inflation.)*

Lesson Checkpoint

Text: Self-Check, text page 311
Answers

1. The most important job of the Federal Reserve is to maintain a stable supply of money.
2. Changes in the reserve requirement have a very large effect on the economy; therefore, the Board of Governors initiates such changes as infrequently as possible.
3. The Fed uses monetary policy to stabilize the economy.

Follow-up Assignments   (Independent Practice/Extension/Homework)

1. Text: Applying What You Have Learned, text page 311
   Answers

   a. If the Fed increases the discount rate, banks will be less likely to borrow from the Fed and the money in circulation will decrease.
   b. If the Fed lowers the reserve requirement, banks will have to keep less money in reserve, loans will increase, and the money in circulation will also increase.
   c. If the Fed buys government bonds, bank deposits will go up as the bonds are paid for and the money in circulation will also increase.
   d. If the Fed sells government bonds, bank deposits will go down to pay for the bonds and the money in circulation will also decrease.

e. If the Fed raises the reserve requirement, banks will have to keep more money on reserve, loans will decrease, and the money in circulation will also decrease.

f. If the Fed lowers the discount rate, banks will be more likely to borrow from the Fed and the amount of money in circulation will increase.

2. Ask your students to take a survey of five adults. They should ask each person what the Federal Reserve System does. Then they should ask how much the person would care if interest rates for consumer loans went up 5 percent. Ask students to report the results of their survey to the class. It would not be surprising to find that many people who believe interest rates are important know little about the Federal Reserve System.

Section Evaluation

Self-Check, text page 311
Understanding Economics, questions 9–10
(Chapter 11 Review, text pages 314–316)

ADDITIONAL MATERIALS FOR CHAPTER 11

Chapter Evaluation

Teacher's Resource Binder: Chapter 11 Quiz

Reteaching and Extension

See the *Teacher's Resource Binder* and the *Student Activity Guide* for additional handouts and activities for Chapter 11.

TEACHER'S BIBLIOGRAPHY FOR CHAPTER 11

Economics Sources

Doty, Richard G. *Money of the World.* New York: Grosset and Dunlap, 1978. A short

history of coins and currency that is suitable for the average or below-average pupil.

The Federal Reserve System: Purposes and Functions, 7th ed. Washington, D.C.: Board of Governors of the Federal Reserve System, 1984. A good explanation of the organization and functions of the United States Central Banking system.

Galbraith, John Kenneth. *Money: Whence It Came, Where It Went.* Boston: Houghton Mifflin, 1975. History of the effects of money on the economy.

Gordon, Sanford D., and Dawson, George G. *Introductory Economics*, 6th ed. Lexington, Mass.: D. C. Heath and Co., 1987. Using simple visuals, Chapters 13 and 14 provide a clear picture of the relationship of the money supply and prices. The Chapter on the "Fed" introduces conflicts in the use of monetary policy.

Open Market Operations. Federal Reserve Bank of New York, 1985. Leads the reader through a typical day's open market operations as the Federal Reserve formulates and implements monetary policy. 49 pages.

References for Additional Teaching Strategies

See the Federal Reserve Systems, *Public Information Materials*, Federal Reserve Bank of New York, 33 Liberty Street, New York, NY 10045, for a comprehensive guide to materials available from the entire system. Teaching materials are listed on pages 26 through 33.

Morton, John, et al. *High School Economics Courses.* New York: Joint Council on Economic Education, 1985. See Lesson 18, "How the Federal Reserve Controls the Money Supply." Handout on the Fed and monetary policy.

You're Accountable. New York State Banking Department and Cornell University. A 50-

minute videotape, with a 36-page instructor's workbook, on saving, spending, and borrowing from the point of view of consumers making choices.

CHAPTER 11 REVIEW ANSWERS

Building Your Vocabulary   (text page 315)

1. FDIC
2. liabilities
3. assets
4. inflation
5. expansion of money
6. money
7. functions of money
8. characteristics of money
9. deflation
10. fiat money
11. reserve requirement
12. discount rate
13. The Federal Reserve System
14. pro-cyclical
15. countercyclical
16. monetary policy
17. open market operations
18. money supply

Understanding Economics   (text page 316)

1. A gold ring would not work well as money because it would not have a uniformly agreed upon value; it would not be accepted by all people; and we do not know how much it will be worth in the future.

2. If the money supply increased by 50 percent, prices would also go up because there would be more dollars trying to buy about the same number of goods and services.

3. If a person put $100 in a checking ac-

count, the bank would be required to keep $12 on reserve. It could lend out the remaining $88.

4. If the bank loaned out the $88, this money would be spent and eventually redeposited into the banking system. This deposit would then become the basis for additional loans, spending, and deposits. This is called the expansion of money.

5. The expansion process can be controlled by the Fed by changing the reserve requirement on checking deposits or by changing the amount of money available for new deposits.

6. If banks were not regulated by the Fed, they would act in a pro-cyclical way. In a recession, they would be able to make few loans. In an expansion, they would make many loans. This would make both the recessions and expansions larger than they would have been.

7. The FDIC insures deposits in banks. If the bank fails and is unable to repay depositors, the FDIC will. In 1987, for example, the FDIC could repay depositors up to $100,000. This encourages people to put their savings into banks where it can be loaned to other people.

8. A bank's assets would typically include cash, securities, loans, and real estate (including its offices). A bank's liabilities would typically include checking and saving deposits, borrowings, and stockholders' equity.

9. The decision-making body within the Federal Reserve System is the Board of Governors.

10. The Fed can carry out monetary policy by

   a. changing the reserve requirement or the percentage of deposits that banks must keep on reserve.

b. changing the discount rate or the percentage of interest banks pay when they borrow from the Fed.

c. buying or selling government securities in open market operations, which regulates the amount of money banks have in order to expand.

Thinking Critically About Economics
(text page 316)

1. It would be hard to use the land as the basis for paying for school unless it was sold and converted into cash. The land does not have a universally agreed upon value. Not everyone would want the land, and there is no way to determine its future worth.

2. Drawings should clearly demonstrate the students' understanding of the relationship between the amount of money in circulation, the quantity of products offered for sale, and the price levels.

3. The $500 deposit in a checking account can be expanded because the bank will have to keep 12 percent on reserve. The other 88 percent can be loaned out. Loans would be spent and money redeposited in the banking system. This would permit other banks to make additional loans which would support still more spending and deposits. The process would continue until total deposits had grown by several thousand dollars.

4. If the reserve requirement was increased to 14 percent, banks would have to keep larger reserves so each step in the expansion process would be smaller. The total amount of money put into circulation by the process would also be smaller.

5. If there were no FDIC, many people would be afraid to deposit their money into banks. This would reduce both the ability of banks to make loans and the amount of money in circulation.

6. If the discount rate was increased by 2 percent, fewer banks would choose to borrow from the Fed. This would reduce the amount of money in circulation.

Special Skills Projects   (text page 316)

1. Your students will discover that the interest rates are not very different. Those banks that offer higher rates are often those that are new to an area, are trying to grow, or have been in financial difficulty and have to pay higher rates to attract deposits.

2. If you can arrange for a loan officer of a bank to speak to your students, it would be both educational and helpful to their own financial future.

CHAPTER 12

Government Decisions and Economic Success (text pages 318–355)

SECTION A.   Government Spending and Jobs (text pages 322–330)

Objectives   (Lesson Focus)

Upon completion of this section, students will be able to:

■ Recognize and explain the basic beliefs of the Classical Economic Theory.

■ Describe how government involvement in the economic system increased after the Great Depression of the 1930s.

■ Contrast the ideas of John Maynard Keynes with those of John Baptiste Say.

■ Define and explain the meaning of fiscal policy.

■ Define, give examples of, and explain

both automatic and discretionary fiscal policy.

- Describe various weaknesses in Keynesian economic policy; in particular, the crowding-out effect and the difficulty of dealing with inflation and unemployment at the same time.

Preparation   (Instruction: Pre-teaching—Vocabulary or Activity)

1. Discussion   Introduce this section by reading the following quotation from the Employment Act of 1946:

> [the federal government should] use all practical means . . . to promote maximum employment, production, and purchasing power.

Explain that although this quotation shows the law sets an objective for government policy, it *does not* require the government to find a job for everyone who wants to work.

Ask your students if they feel the government should guarantee a job to everyone who wants to work. How much would it cost to provide about 7 million jobs (the number of unemployed people in 1987)? Would this force taxes up too much? If everyone was guaranteed a job, would people feel less pressure to work hard? Try to reach a consensus among your students over what the proper role for the government should be in providing jobs to people who are out of work.

Another related question that could be discussed is whether or not everyone who receives government aid and is able to work should be required to work, and if so, how much choice should a person have in the type of work they choose to do?

2. The Personal Narrative   The Personal Narrative for Section A describes how one

family benefited from a job training program provided by the federal government. The subject of the Narrative is a young woman whose widowed mother supported a family of five by working in a shirt factory until it closed. The family lived on welfare benefits for years. Finally the mother found a job working for a government training program. Although the woman's family was helped through the program, she doubts that it will accomplish its objectives for many other people.

The Narrative demonstrates accomplishments and problems that may result from government programs intended to help the poor.

Teaching Suggestions   (Modeling/Guided Practice)

1. Ask your students to pretend they own a factory that makes chairs. It costs them $15 to make a chair. They would like to sell the chairs for $25. There is a major recession in the nation's economy and sales have been very poor. The firm lowered the price of its chairs to $20, but sales did not pick up much. It has been determined by market research that the firm could sell all of its chairs at $14 each. Ask your students whether they would sell their chairs at $14, or close down the factory, store the chairs they have, and wait for prices to go up.

   Next, ask your students to imagine that they worked for the same business under the same conditions. They have a contract that entitles them to a wage of $7.50 an hour. Their manager asks them to accept $5.50 per hour. Remind them that they have mortgage payments to make, children to feed, and need a new car. Ask your students if they would be willing to take a cut in pay.

With the discussion of this situation in mind, ask your students to explain why Say's law didn't work at the beginning of the Great Depression.

2. Ask your students what would happen in each of the following cases (the correct answers, according to J. M. Keynes, have been underlined):

   a. People become convinced that a major recession is about to happen so they decide to save (<u>more</u> or less) out of their current income.

   b. Because of this, they spend (more or <u>less</u>) than they otherwise would have.

   c. Total business sales therefore go (up or <u>down</u>).

   d. Business inventories start to (<u>increase</u> or decrease).

   e. This causes businesses to (<u>lay off</u> or hire more) workers.

   f. As a result, total income for all workers goes (up or <u>down</u>).

   g. The workers who have lost their jobs are unable to save anything, so total savings for all workers goes (up or <u>down</u>).

   h. By trying to save more, workers as a group have actually ended up saving (more or <u>less</u>) and national income has gone (up or <u>down</u>).

   Explain that Keynes called this idea the "Paradox of Thrift." When society as a whole tried to save more, it ended up saving less, because sales would go down, people would be laid off, and would not be able to save at all. Keynes said the government should increase its spending when people become worried and spend less. He claimed that this would keep total spending and employment at a steady rate and would reduce the effects of a recession.

3. To illustrate a limitation on Keynesian policy, ask students to complete the story in Discussion Topic 18 from the *Teacher's Resource Binder*. Read some of the better papers in class and discuss them.

   After your students discuss their paragraphs, point out that this is essentially what happened in the United States from 1982 to 1983. The economist Milton Friedman said that it took so long for the government to act that the country would be better off if Congress didn't try to carry out discretionary fiscal policy. By the time jobs were created by the new tax, the economy was already on the road to recovery.

Lesson Checkpoint

Text:　Self-Check, text page 330
　　　　Answers

1. Classical economists believed the market economy would end a recession by lowering prices, interest rates, and wages.

2. Keynes believed that in a recession, the government should help the market along by spending more money than it took in from tax revenues.

3. Discretionary policy requires a choice of specific action to go into effect, whereas automatic fiscal policy does not.

4. The action chosen may take place too long after the economic event, thus rendering the remedial action ineffective.

Follow-up Assignments　(Independent Practice/Extension/Homework)

Text: Applying What You Have Learned,
text page 330
Answers

*Strengths of Government-Sponsored
Job Training Program*

1. These programs offer job training
and/or retraining whereby formerly unemployed workers can
acquire skills to enhance their
future employability.

2. These programs decrease government spending and taxes to support welfare and unemployment
compensation programs.

*Weaknesses of Government-
Sponsored Job Training Program*

1. Often the type of job-training
programs offered to workers are
impractical, because work in that
field does not exist in their local
area.

2. The government spending that is
required to fund these programs
often conflicts with attempts to
fight inflation and to keep interest
rates down.

Section Evaluation

Self-Check, text page 330
Understanding Economics, questions 1–4
(Chapter 12 Review, text pages 352–354)

SECTION B.   Government Policies and Inflation (text pages 332–337)

Objectives   (Lesson Focus)

Upon completion of this section, students
will be able to:

- Describe attempts by the federal government to regulate prices and/or wages.
- Explain why government price controls
may cause shortages.

Preparation   (Instruction: Pre-teaching—
Vocabulary or Activity)

1. Discussion   Introduce this section by
asking students how they would react to a
ten-percent rate of inflation if they lived on a
fixed income of $645 a month and had the
following expenses. Give each student a copy
of the list in Discussion Topic 19 from the
Teacher's Resource Binder and ask them where
they would, or could, cut back.

Point out that even if students stop set-
ting aside money for savings, they still would
need an income next year of $682 a month
just to buy the same things they are buying
now. Ask your students where they would be
forced to cut back. If the inflation went on
year after year while their income remained
unchanged, what would eventually happen?
Use this exercise to demonstrate the importance of controlling inflation for people on a
fixed income.

2. The Personal Narrative   The Personal
Narrative in Section B describes how various
people are affected by inflation. The subject
of the Narrative is a young woman whose
grandmother is adversely affected by inflation because she lives on a fixed income. The
young woman is planning to attend a junior
college and faces increased transportation,
tuition, and book expenses. Her father dis-
covers that his property taxes are about to be
increased. All of these people wonder why
the government has not been able to limit
inflation.

The Narrative demonstrates the need that
many people feel for more effective government control over inflation.

Teaching Suggestions   (Modeling/Guided
Practice)

1. Ask your students to pretend they trap
lobsters for a living. Lobster fishermen

have dangerous jobs and work hard. They expect to earn a good income. Lobsters have recently been selling for $7 a pound, and their price has gone up about 10 percent per year. Even so, many lobster fishermen have given up their jobs for other employment in recent years.

Suppose the government passed a law that said lobsters could not be sold for more than $5 a pound. This would make it impossible for lobster fishermen to earn more than $20,000 a year after they had paid all of their expenses. Ask your students how they would answer each of the following questions under such conditions:

a. What would happen to the number of lobster fishermen who would consider looking for other work?

b. What would happen to the number of lobster fishermen who would choose to invest in new boats and equipment?

c. What would happen to the supply of lobsters offered for sale over the next year or two?

d. What would happen to the number of people who would want to buy lobsters when the government forced fishermen to lower their prices to $5 per pound?

e. What problem would be caused by the government price control?

Use this example to discuss why government price controls have often led to shortages of products.

2. Discuss whether special tax breaks for elderly people are fair. Many local governments allow older people to reduce the assessed value of their property by a specified amount when they figure their property tax. Bus fares and other public services are often reduced for elderly people. They receive special consideration when they pay their income taxes. In addition to these special considerations, older people receive substantial aid from the government that is paid for by other taxpayers. Do your students support giving elderly people special treatment if it means higher taxes for other people? Why or why not?

3. The rates that public utilities are allowed to charge for electricity are set by state regulatory agencies. Such utilities operate with what is essentially a form of government price control. Many people would like to see rate requests turned down or limited. Discuss how a public utility could react to a lack of rate increases when its costs had increased. Which of the following possibilities do your students feel would be most likely? How would customers be affected by each of the following possible actions?

a. Stop paying interest on loans and dividends to stockholders. (A utility that did not pay interest could be forced into bankruptcy by its creditors. The mere possibility of such a decision would cause a utility to pay higher interest rates for money it needs to borrow. This could cause a need for even higher rates in the future.)

b. Spend less on service to its customers.

c. Spend less on investing in new equipment and replacing equipment that wears out.

d. Reduce employee salaries and benefits.

e. Reduce the number of employees.

Point out that the long-range effect of many of these decisions would hurt customers. There could be a shortage of electrical power in the future that could cost people their jobs and hurt the area's economy.

Lesson Checkpoint

Text: Self-Check, text page 337
Answers

1. Most economists consider fiscal policy to be more effective in the control of demand-pull inflation.
2. Government price regulation has often resulted in product shortages.
3. Pressure on the government to regulate prices has lessened in recent years.

Follow-up Assignments (Independent Practice/Extension/Homework)

Text: Applying What You Have Learned, text page 337
Answers

There are many possible answers that could be given by students. Each answer should be graded according to the logic and basis of support provided. Three potential problems created by the enactment of a law that would limit prices charged to the elderly could include:

1. People under 65 could be forced to pay more to make up for those over 65 who pay less.
2. Fewer goods and services might be ordered for those over 65.
3. The government would have to spend more money to enforce the law.

Section Evaluation

Self-Check, text page 337

Understanding Economics, questions 5–7 (Chapter 12 Review, text pages 352–354)

SECTION C. Supply-Side Economics (text pages 338–342)

Objectives (Lesson Focus)

Upon completion of this section, students will be able to:

- Explain why supply-side economists feel that it is possible to deal with inflation and unemployment at the same time by lowering costs of production.
- Describe methods that supply-side economists would use to reduce costs and adjust the location of the supply curve.
- Identify and explain various supply-side policies that have been carried out by the federal government.

Preparation (Instruction: Pre-teaching—Vocabulary or Activity)

1. Discussion Introduce this section by copying the following lists on the chalkboard. The list on the left is made up of benefits of supply-side policies that have been put into effect by the federal government. The list on the right is made up of costs that are associated with these changes. Discuss the difference between the types of people who would have benefited from, and those who would have paid the costs of, these supply-side policies.

Benefits

Income taxes are lower.
Businesses that invested in new equipment received tax breaks.
People who saved in IRAs paid lower taxes.
People who made profits in the stock market paid lower taxes on these profits.

Costs

It became more difficult to qualify for food stamps.

There were reductions in government-supported day-care centers.

Federal employees did not receive wage increases in some years.

There was a reduction in federal support for low-income housing.

Your students will recognize that the benefits of these policies have gone largely to people with relatively high incomes, while the immediate costs have been paid by people with lower incomes. Explain why supply-side economists believe these results are justified in the long run.

Supply-side economists believe improved standards of living can be provided to all people over time by increasing the incentives to save and invest in more efficient means of production. People with lower incomes may lose some government benefits in the short run, but they are expected to be able to find better jobs in the future.

2. The Personal Narrative The Personal Narrative in Section C describes the effect of supply-side economic policy on different individuals. The subject of the Narrative is a young man who has been disabled in an accident. He has a low income and high medical expenses. As a result, he pays almost no federal income tax, although he benefits from many programs that are supported through federal funds. He is concerned that attempts to cut taxes and reduce social programs will hurt him. He does not understand why people who are financially secure should benefit from changes in the law which would harm people who are poor or disabled.

The Narrative demonstrates trade-offs between the costs and benefits of implementing supply-side economic policy. It shows the conflicting values that are related to this problem.

Teaching Suggestions (Modeling/Guided Practice)

Ask your students to pretend they run a large business that produces toys. Ask them how they would react to each of the following events:

Event	
Would they choose to make more toys?	**Would this cause them to raise or lower prices?**
Yes/No	Raise/Lower
Tax deductions cause them to buy equipment that allows them to use 10% less labor.	_____ _____
The tax rate on their profit is reduced from 46% to 34%.	_____ _____
Interest rates they must pay to borrow money go down when people are encouraged to save more in IRA accounts.	_____ _____
They find that more people are willing to work for them at lower wages when social benefit programs are reduced.	_____ _____

Point out that all of these ideas were placed into law under the Reagan administration in the 1980s.

Lesson Checkpoint

Text: Self-Check, text page 342

Answers

1. Traditional Keynesian policy is designed to change demand.

2. Supply-side economists believe that reduced taxes can encourage people to save money.

3. Supply-side economists believe that greater investment increases productivity.

Follow-up Assignments (Independent Practice/Extension/Homework)

Text: Applying What You Have Learned, text page 342
        Answers

1. Additional research could be carried out by firms that benefited from the lower taxes. This research might find a way to help the young man in the Narrative.

2. A stronger economy that could result from the tax cuts could provide a better job for the young man.

Section Evaluation

Self-Check, text page 342
Understanding Economics, questions 8 and 9 (Chapter 12 Review, text pages 352–354)

SECTION D.   Government Social Programs (text pages 343–348)

Objectives   (Lesson Focus)

Upon completion of this section, students will be able to:

- Explain the meaning of the "misery index."
- Describe the basic characteristics of government social programs, including Social Security, unemployment compensation, and welfare.

Preparation   (Instruction: Pre-teaching—Vocabulary or Activity)

1. Discussion   Introduce this section by giving each student a 3-by-5 card. Tell them not to put their names on the cards. Students should imagine that they are currently thirty years old, have a family with three children, and earn roughly $30,000 a year of which they pay $7,200 in all types of taxes. Ask them to answer each of the following questions:

a. Would you support greater aid for the nation's poor?

b. Would you be willing to pay more taxes to help the poor?

c. How much of your income would you contribute each year to help the poor?

d. What do you believe is the single most important thing the government could do to help reduce poverty?

Discuss your students' answers. Why would some students support greater aid while others would not? What suggestions were made to reduce poverty? Were they realistic?

2. The Personal Narrative   The Personal Narrative in Section D describes a young man's reaction to his first personal contact with people who live in poverty. The subject of the Narrative lives in an affluent suburb but has volunteered to cook and deliver food to a city mission in a poor urban area. He is surprised to find that people who use the mission come from many backgrounds. He recognizes his good fortune in having been born in a family that has income and wealth and wonders why more has not been done to help poor people.

The Narrative describes different groups that often experience poverty in the United States and raises the question of determining society's degree of responsibility to these people.

Teaching Suggestions   (Modeling/Guided Practice)

1. Discuss whether your students believe unemployment compensation and welfare should be run by the federal government—as with Social Security—instead of by each state. Help your students make one list of advantages that could result from putting these programs under federal control and a second list of

problems that could be caused by federal control. Possible items for each list are found below.

Possible Advantages of Federal Control

(1) There would be equal benefits throughout the country.
(2) Tax burdens would be better equalized.
(3) There would be less reason for poor people to move to different areas to obtain more benefits.
(4) It would reduce the possibility of local political patronage in these programs.

Possible Disadvantages of Federal Control

(1) There would be equal benefits regardless of differences in the cost of living.
(2) Money would be taken from areas that were successful and sent to less successful areas.
(3) There would be a reason for poor people to move to areas with low costs of living.
(4) It would provide even greater political power to the federal government.

2. Some people have suggested institutionalizing people who are unable to take care of themselves because of mental, emotional, or other problems. They believe people who have no home should be placed in shelters and cared for regardless of their individual wishes. Others believe that society should not take personal freedoms from people simply because they live on the street. If the government required institutionalization for such people, it would cost billions of dollars every year. Discuss this issue with your students. Do they feel this idea would be morally correct and/or economically possible? Can they think of alternative plans to solve the problem of our nation's homeless?

Lesson Checkpoint

Text: Self-Check, text page 348
   Answers

1. The Social Security Act of 1935 created programs for retirement benefits, unemployment insurance, and welfare.
2. The trends toward smaller families and longer life expectancy have put pressures on the Social Security system.
3. State-administered programs include unemployment insurance and welfare. Federally-administered programs include Social Security and Medicare.

Follow-up Assignments   (Independent Practice/Extension/Homework)

1. Text: Applying What You Have Learned, text page 348
   Answers

   a. Relatively few welfare recipients could work for their benefits. Whether or not those recipients who are able to work should be required to do so is a value judgment.
   b. Cuts in welfare benefits would probably increase the number of recipients who are looking for work; however, many would not be able to work under any conditions because they are too young, too old, or disabled.

c. The people who would be most hurt by a cut in benefits are those who could not support themselves. Many of these people would be young, old, or disabled.

2. People of different age groups often have varying opinions on Social Security taxes. Assign each of your students to ask the following question to at least one working person in each of the following age groups: 20 to 25, 30 to 35, 40 to 45, and 50 to 55. Tell them to report their findings to the class. Discuss possible reasons for any differences between the answers provided by the age groups. Question: "Would you support increasing the Social Security tax to guarantee that Social Security benefits are kept at their present level?"

3. Teacher's Resource Binder: Critical Thinking Activity, Chapter 12 (answers in Binder).

Section Evaluation

Self-Check, text page 348
Understanding Economics, questions 10 and 11 (Chapter 12 Review, text pages 352–354)

ADDITIONAL MATERIALS FOR CHAPTER 12

Chapter Evaluation

Teacher's Resource Binder: Chapter 12 Quiz

Reteaching and Extension

See the *Teacher's Resource Binder* and the *Student Activity Guide* for additional handouts and activities for Chapter 12.

TEACHER'S BIBLIOGRAPHY FOR CHAPTER 12

Economics Sources

Cagen, Phillip, ed. *Essay in Contemporary Eco-nomic Problems: the Economy in Deficit.* Washington, D.C.: American Enterprise Institute, 1985. Presents differing viewpoints about deficit financing and the impact of the debt.

Gordon, Sanford D., and Dawson, George G. *Introductory Economics*, 6th ed. Lexington, Mass.: 1987. See Chapter 15, "Formulating Modern Economic Policy," for an evaluation of classical, Keynesian, neo-Keynesian, supply-side, monetarist and rational expansionist's positions for stabilizing the economy at full employment without inflation.

Hailstones, Thomas J. *A Guide to Supply-Side Economics.* Richmond, Va.: Robert F. Dame, Inc., 1982. A brief review of the supply-side, or Reaganomic, position.

Lekachman, Robert. *Reaganomics: Greed Is Not Enough.* New York: Pantheon Books, 1982. A critique on Reagan's economic policies by a neo-Keynesian.

Rosen, Daniel. *Debt and Deficit.* New York: Federal Reserve Bank of New York, 1985. An 18-page pamphlet that explains the public debt and its impact in clear and simple terms.

Stein, Herbert. *Presidential Economics: the Making of Economic Policy from Roosevelt to Reagan and Beyond.* New York: Simon and Schuster, 1984. Reviews stabilization policies of nine presidents and suggests a consensus policy from a former chairman of the Council of Economic Advisers.

References for Additional Teaching Strategies

Inflation-Recession-Depression.   Prentice-Hall Media, Inc., 1975. Four filmstrips, each 12 minutes, with cassettes or records and teacher's guide on the causes and consequences of inflation, recessions, and various economic policies to deal with them.

Morton, John, et al. *High School Economics*

Courses. New York: Joint Council on Economic Education, 1985. See Lesson 14, "Economic Ups and Downs"; Lesson 15, "Economic Goals"; and Lesson 19, "Analyzing Fiscal Policy."

CHAPTER 12 REVIEW ANSWERS

Building Your Vocabulary   (text page 353)

1. crowding-out effect
2. misery index
3. AFDC
4. Social Security Act
5. indexed
6. laissez-faire
7. John Baptiste Say
8. John Maynard Keynes
9. Phase II
10. concessionary contracts
11. fiscal policy
12. classical economics
13. IRA
14. supply-side economics
15. automatic stabilization
16. discretionary fiscal policy
17. Employment Act of 1946

Understanding Economics   (text pages 353–354)

1. Classical economists believed that in a recession prices, wages, and interest rates would fall, which would bring the recession to an end.
2. Keynes identified spending that supported personal consumption, business investment, and the government.
3. During a recession, according to Keynes, the government could bring about higher spending levels by either increasing government spending without increasing taxes or by cutting taxes without cutting government spending.
4. Automatic fiscal policy, such as unemployment compensation, requires no new or special action by the government to go into effect. In contrast, discretionary fiscal policy does require new action by the government. Increases in federal tax on gasoline is an example of discretionary fiscal policy.
5. Increased spending by the government to fight unemployment could contribute to higher rates of inflation.
6. Decreased spending by the government to fight inflation could contribute to higher rates of unemployment.
7. Many people felt that President Nixon's Phase II regulations were an unnecessary intrusion by the government into the free market. They often argued that the policy would result in the misallocation of resources.
8. According to supply-side economists, if firms produce more goods and services, there will be more jobs and less need to increase prices.
9. Some supply-side economists argue that tax cuts which benefit people in high income brackets will enable them to invest in new factories and equipment. Tax cuts that go to the poor are more likely to be used for consumption.
10. The benefits paid for welfare and unemployment compensation are different in each state. It is possible that people have chosen to move to states that have relatively higher payments. This may have created a concentration of less affluent people in these states.
11. Private programs are limited to the ability and willingness of people to give. In areas where there are many poor people, there will probably be fewer people who

are able and willing to help them than in areas that are more affluent.

Thinking Critically About Economics
(text page 354)

1. The following three factors, or circumstances, have changed to increase the role of the government in the economy:

   a. The products sold now are much more complicated.

   b. The size of businesses now are much larger.

   c. The number of goods consumers now have to deal with is much larger.

2. In a recession, a classical economist would want the government to run a balanced budget and wait for the economy to adjust itself. A Keynesian economist would want the government to increase its spending or cut taxes to increase the amount of total spending and create more jobs. A supply-side economist would want the government to reduce taxes to provide firms with more money to invest in increasing their productivity.

3. This event shows that it often takes a long time to carry out discretionary fiscal policy. The additional spending was needed in 1981–1982, but it did not actually take place until the end of 1983. By that time, the economy was already recovering. A tax cut would probably have taken almost as much time to put into effect. The only part that might have taken less time would have been the time needed for people to spend the money after their taxes had been cut.

4. Additional government borrowing could force interest rates up from what they otherwise would have been. Higher interest rates will discourage people and businesses from borrowing and spending. Therefore, the additional government spending could result in less personal consumption spending and business investment.

Special Skills Project   (text page 354)

Your students will probably find that the welfare forms require a fairly high degree of sophistication and understanding to complete. They will also find that the forms ask for a significant amount of personal information that some people might not want to provide.

PART 3 REVIEW ANSWERS

Understanding Economic Concepts
(text pages 357–358)

1. The answer is provided as an example in the text.

2. It is difficult to measure the GNP accurately because many goods and services are produced and not reported to the government in the *underground economy*.

3. *Durable goods* are products that last a long time and tend to be expensive. Firms that produce these goods are hurt more than other firms in an economic downturn because they are expensive and customers often put off buying these items in a recession.

4. The government publishes a list of *leading indicators* each month, made up of factors that tend to change before the rest of the economy. By studying these indicators businesses are often able to make accurate predictions of economic trends in the near future.

5. Many important products would be too expensive for people to afford individually if they were not provided as *public*

goods and services by the government. Examples include roads, schools, and national defense.

6. A *negative externality* occurs when a third party who is not the producer or consumer of a product pays a cost associated with the production of that product. Pollution of our water is a common example of this. When the government forces a firm to stop polluting a river, it is attempting to correct a negative externality.

7. A *benefits-received* tax is placed on those who use the public good or service that is supported by the tax they pay. An *ability-to-pay* tax is placed on those who are most able to support public goods and services.

8. *Pork barrel legislation* is government spending that is intended to help elected government officials keep their offices by supporting projects which benefit people in their elective districts.

9. Federal income taxes are *progressive* because people who have larger taxable incomes pay a larger percentage of their income in taxes than those with smaller taxable incomes. Most state and local taxes are *regressive* because people who have larger incomes often pay a smaller percentage of their income in taxes than those with smaller incomes.

10. *Frictional unemployment* is made up of people who have been out of work for only a short time.

    Seasonal unemployment is made up of people who have been laid off because their jobs only exist during one part of the year.

    Cyclical unemployment is made up of people who have been laid off because of a recession or a downturn in the economy.

    Structural unemployment is made up

of people who have been laid off because their skills or abilities are no longer in demand.

11. There are two basic types of inflation. *Demand-pull inflation* occurs when people try to buy more goods than there are goods offered for sale. The resulting shortage forces prices up. *Cost-push inflation* occurs when firms try to pass increased costs of production on to customers in the form of higher prices.

12. *Poverty* is a relative term and is defined by comparing what most people in a group have with the smaller amount that those who live in poverty have. In the United States, people who are unemployed often suffer from poverty and this situation may be made worse by inflation.

13. The three functions of money are to serve as a:

    ■ *medium of exchange*, providing units of value which allow transactions to take place.

    ■ *measure of value*, providing a method of comparing the value of different products offered for sale.

    ■ *store of value*, providing a method of accumulating or saving value at one time to be used in the future.

14. When banks receive new deposits of cash, they are required by law to keep a set percentage of the deposit on hand in reserve. They may loan out the remainder, which will be borrowed, spent, and redeposited in the banking system. This new deposit becomes the basis of repeated loans, spending, and deposits. Economists call these transactions the *expansion process*.

15. Federal Reserve System steps to regulate the money supply that are intended to

stabilize the economic system make up what is called *monetary policy*.

16. To regulate the money supply and carry out monetary policy the Federal Reserve System may:

   - change the *reserve requirement* or percentage of deposits banks are required to keep on hand.
   - change the *discount rate* or percentage of interest charged to banks that borrow funds from the Federal Reserve System.
   - buy or sell government securities in *open market operations*, which will adjust the level of deposits in banks.

17. If banks were not regulated by the Fed they would probably follow *pro-cyclical* policies. In recessions, they would find it difficult to make many loans, causing the recession to be deeper. In an expansion, they would be able to make many loans, making the expansion greater.

18. The *Federal Deposit Insurance Corporation* was established in the Great Depression to insure deposits and restore confidence in the nation's banking system.

19. *Keynesian economic theory* suggests that it is possible to stabilize the economic system by adjusting the government's taxing, spending, and budget deficit, to create enough total spending to supply jobs for all people who want to work.

20. During the administration of Ronald Reagan, many government policies were based on *supply-side economics*. These policies were intended to encourage greater saving and investment, reduce costs of production, improve efficiency, and create more jobs.

Writing About Economics   (text pages 358–359)

1. Students' answers should reflect an understanding of the meaning of the *gross national product* and the three methods of measuring the GNP: the *income approach*, the *expenditures approach*, and the *production approach*.

2. Students' answers should reflect an understanding of the three economic concepts identified in the question by explaining the costs and benefits associated with each of the three possible plans. The first plan relates most closely to the *productivity principle* of taxation in that it is intended to encourage business growth and an expansion of production. The second plan relates to the *ability-to-pay-principle* of taxation in that it would reduce taxes for those who own property. Allowing the firms to bury waste on public land would probably result in *negative externalities*.

3. Students' answers should reflect an understanding of the costs and benefits associated with implementing *supply-side economic* policies. People who are relatively well-off would benefit most directly from the reduced taxes. People who are relatively poor would be hurt most directly by reduced government services.

Discussing Economics   (text pages 359–360)

1. Students should identify the issue(s) involved in limiting the government's ability to tax and should clearly state whether or not they support the idea. Students should clearly explain the costs and benefits associated with the plan and why they believe their answer is best.

2. Students should identify the issue(s) involved in simply giving people who

live in poverty enough money to bring them above the poverty level and should clearly state whether or not they support the idea. Students should clearly explain the costs and benefits associated with the plan and why they believe their answer is best.

3. Students should identify the issue(s) involved in requiring banks to make a share of their loans to minority owned businesses and should clearly state whether or not they support the idea. Students should clearly explain the costs and benefits associated with the plan and why they believe their answer is best.

Problem-Solving in Economics

Chapter 8   (text page 360)

1. Items listed by students may be things that did not exist when their parents were young or things their parents could not afford.

2. Items listed by students that do not involve money are likely to be related to their family, friendships, or to nature.

3. Student answers will reflect their individual values and should be given credit as long as they are explained in a logical way.

4. a. A decrease in new building permits indicates a downturn in construction.

   b. Lower interest rates should encourage borrowing and spending.

   c. Working longer hours indicates greater production and income, which should bring about greater spending.

   d. Slower deliveries indicates more customers and steady employment.

   e. Reduced saving rates reflect greater

spending and probably consumer confidence in the economy.

   f. Few new businesses being started indicates reduced confidence in the future and probably a slower creation of new jobs.

Chapter 9   (text page 361)

1. These are only some of many possible correct answers.

   a. A person who owns land on the river might support the idea because it should increase the value of his property.

   b. A person who owns a farm on the other side of town would probably oppose the idea because he would receive little benefit from it.

   c. A person who owns a bait shop would probably support the idea because it should increase the number of customers he has.

   d. A person who owns a house on the river and likes peace and quiet would probably oppose the idea because it would increase the traffic on the river.

   e. A person who owns a factory along the river would probably oppose the idea because he would not benefit directly from it, and it could increase public pressure to reduce any pollution the factory might be creating.

2. Answers that are reasonably close to those below should be accepted.

   a. Roughly 26 percent of federal spending went to payments to individuals in 1960.

   b. Roughly 45 percent of federal spending went to payments to individuals in 1986.

   c. Roughly 49 percent of federal spending went to national defense in 1960.

d. Roughly 27 percent of federal spending went to national defense in 1986.

e. The proportions of federal spending that went to payments to individuals and national defense were roughly reversed between 1960 and 1986. The payments to individuals grew while national defense spending fell as a percentage of the total.

f. The part of the federal budget that went to pay interest on the national debt roughly doubled between 1960 and 1986.

Chapter 10   (text page 362)

1. a. Joe is cyclically unemployed because he was laid off when his employer's sales went down.

b. Max is frictionally unemployed because he is moving between jobs with the expectation of finding a better job soon.

c. Jan is seasonally unemployed because she was laid off after the Christmas season.

d. Sue is structurally unemployed because her employer no longer needs her skill. A computer is doing her work instead.

e. Ted is structurally unemployed because he does not have the skills possessed by the college graduate.

2. Students' answers will vary. Most of their answers will probably involve interpersonal relations, families, and self-respect.

3. Students' answers will vary. Their explanations should demonstrate logical thinking and a consideration of the costs and benefits of each alternative.

4. Students' answers will vary. Their suggestions and explanations should demonstrate logical thinking.

Chapter 11   (text pages 362–363)

1. a. When money is saved, it is a store of value.

b. When money is used to buy something, it is a medium of exchange.

c. When you shop where prices are lowest, money is used as a measure of value.

d. Money that is borrowed has been saved by someone and is therefore a store of value. When a loan is paid back, the money will have value, which shows that it has reasonably stable value over time.

2. a. If the Fed lowers the reserve requirement to 10 percent, it will increase the amount of money in circulation because banks will not have to keep as much money on hand and will be able to make more loans.

b. Reducing the money supply means the same as decreasing the amount of money in circulation.

c. If people hold less cash and make more deposits, banks will have more money to lend. This will increase the amount of money in circulation.

d. If banks decide to hold more cash, they will be able to make fewer loans. This will decrease the amount of money in circulation.

e. Increasing the money supply means the same as increasing the amount of money in circulation.

f. If the Fed raises the reserve requirement to 14 percent, banks will have to keep more money on hand and will be able to make fewer loans, which will reduce the amount of money in circulation.

3. Student answers will vary. They should demonstrate an understanding of the factors that determine the risk associated with lending money. These could include the person's credit history, income, assets they own, and other financial responsibilities.

4. a. In inflation, the Fed is likely to decrease the amount (or rate of growth) of money in circulation.

   b. If there is unemployment, the Fed is likely to increase the amount (or rate of growth) of money in circulation.

   c. It is hard for the Fed to deal with both inflation and unemployment at the same time because it cannot increase and decrease the amount of money in circulation at the same time.

   d. If prices go up because the cost of imported raw materials go up, there is little the Fed can do about it because foreign producers are little effected by the money supply or interest rates in the United States.

   e. If people and businesses are worried about the future, they may choose not to borrow, regardless of how low interest rates are.

   f. It is difficult for the Fed to deal with the problems of (1) inflation and unemployment at the same time because it can't increase and decrease the money supply at the same time;

(2) increased prices of imports because foreign suppliers are not effected by changes in the money supply or interest rates in this country; (3) bad recessions because people and businesses may choose not to borrow and spend money, regardless of how low interest rates are.

Chapter 12   (text page 363)

1. Students' answers will vary. They should address all parts of the question and demonstrate careful thought and the use of logic.

2. Students' answers should address the problems this firm will have in staying in business if it does not increase its prices by more than 6 percent. Students should make use of the facts provided in the question.

3. If there were no programs to help the poor, in a recession:

   a. The poor would have to cut back more on the number of items they purchase than they would have if these programs existed.

   b. The number of foreclosures and repossessions would increase more than they would have if these programs existed.

   c. There would be fewer jobs than there would have been if these existed.

   d. Programs to help the poor also help those people who are not poor or unemployed because they allow the poor to continue spending.

UNDERSTANDING INTERNATIONAL ECONOMICS

CHAPTER 13

Why Countries Trade (text pages 366–389)

SECTION A.   The Benefits of Trade (text pages 369–374)

Objectives   (Lesson Focus)

Upon completion of this section, students will be able to:

- Identify the theories of absolute and comparative advantage, and describe the conclusions that can be drawn from them concerning international trade.
- Define and explain the two basic barriers to trade: tariffs and quotas.
- Describe possible reasons for establishing tariffs or quotas, including: the infant industry argument, the national security argument, the protection of domestic jobs argument, and the maintaining economic stability argument.

Preparation   (Instruction: Pre-teaching—Vocabulary or Activity)

1. Discussion   Introduce this section by asking students how they would react if they were assigned to do tasks with which they were unfamiliar. For example, you could ask students who are uninterested in motorcycles what they would say if they were required to participate in a motorcycle race. Or you could ask students who do not know much about cooking what they would do if they had to bake a cake. Mention tasks that you believe some students in your class will know how to perform.

Remind your students about the terms *specialization* and *division of labor* presented in Section A of Chapter 2. Point out that if students were able to decide who would do each task, they would be able to accomplish the tasks more efficiently, since students could perform the tasks to which they were best suited. The tasks could be completed more quickly and all the students would gain.

Explain that the same concepts can be applied to countries. When countries specialize in making products, they produce more efficiently and only trade for products they do not produce as well. Production becomes more efficient and all nations are better off.

2. The Personal Narrative   The Personal Narrative in Section A describes the benefits that some individuals have received from international trade and compares them with the cost paid by other individuals. The subject of the Narrative is a young man whose father sells imported cars for a living. Many of his friends believe there is something un-American about his father's job. He describes arguments his father uses to answer people who feel selling imports is wrong.

The Narrative demonstrates the trade-offs between the costs and benefits of international trade. It also shows that the people who receive the benefits may not be the same people who pay for the costs of international trade.

Teaching Suggestions   (Modeling/Guided Practice)

Describe the difference between tariffs that were used to raise revenue for our government in the early 1800s and those which have been used, or suggested, more recently to protect American manufacturers. In the early part of our history there was no income tax to support the federal government. Most federal tax revenue came from tariffs and excise taxes. We taxed imports to support the government more often than to control trade. Today tariff revenues are less than 3 percent of the federal budget and are used primarily to regulate trade.

Ask your students what would happen to trade if the government tried to balance the budget by raising tariffs. Remember that our 1985 budget deficit was roughly $220 billion while we imported $345 billion in foreign products that year. Tariffs high enough to balance the budget would so drastically reduce trade that little money would be collected.

Lesson Checkpoint

Text: Self-Check, text page 374
       Answers

1. According to the theories of absolute and comparative advantage, nations should specialize in making the products they are most effective at, and they should trade for their least efficiently produced items.

2. A tariff is a tax on an import; a quota is a limit on the amount of a product a nation will allow to be imported.

3. The infant industry argument suggests that tariffs be used to protect a developing nation's new industries.

Follow-up Assignments   (Independent Practice/Extension/Homework)

Text: Applying What You Have Learned, text page 374
       Answers

1. The *infant industry argument* states that new firms should be protected from more advanced foreign competition with tariffs until they have a chance to grow and become more efficient.

2. The *national security argument* states that we should produce products that are important to our national defense even if they can be purchased for less from other countries. We do not want to be dependent on other countries for things we really need.

3. The *protection of domestic jobs argument* states that we should restrict imports so that American workers will be employed.

4. The *maintaining economic stability argument* states that we should diversify into areas where we are not as efficient as other nations because we do not want to be too dependent on a relatively low number of products.

Section Evaluation

Self-Check, text page 374
Understanding Economics, questions 1–3
   (Chapter 13 Review, text pages 385–387)

SECTION B.   The Costs of Trade (text pages 375–379)

Objectives   (Lesson Focus)

Upon completion of this section, students will be able to:

- Define a positive balance of trade, and describe costs and benefits associated with having a positive balance of trade.

- Describe steps taken or considered by the U.S. government to help individuals and firms harmed by trade, including trade adjustment assistance, laws against dumping, and protectionist legislation.

Preparation　(Instruction: Pre-teaching—Vocabulary or Activity)

1. Discussion　Introduce this section by asking students to identify the make of car their family owns (or closest relative if they don't own a car). Identify each car as an American or foreign brand. Ask students why their family chose to buy that particular type of car. Most of the reasons they give will probably concern *individual* preferences. Help your students to make a second list of results that buying American or foreign cars could have for the economy *as a whole*.

2. The Personal Narrative　The Personal Narrative in Section B describes the effect of foreign competition on an individual firm and its workers. The subject of the story was unemployed for an extended period of time after he was laid off from Atari in 1984. Although he suffered from foreign competition, the worker drives an imported car. He is torn between the costs of foreign competition he has paid and the benefits he receives from buying foreign products.

The Narrative demonstrates trade-offs made by Americans when they buy imported goods.

Teaching Suggestions　(Modeling/Guided Practice)

1. Discuss government purchases of foreign goods. A large northeastern city recently purchased subway cars from a foreign manufacturer. The city's leaders said the foreign cars were about 8 percent less expensive than American cars would

have been. By purchasing foreign cars, they saved the city almost $6 million.

Some people argued that buying foreign cars cost American workers jobs, businesses profits, and our government tax revenues. They believe these considerations are more important than being able to pay a slightly lower price.

Help your students identify issues involved in this situation. Organize a debate over whether or not governments in this country should buy American products even if they do cost more.

2. Point out that there are dangers in counting on foreign producers. Political and economic problems in other countries may interrupt the supply of products that we have come to rely on. For example, in the summer of 1987, civil unrest in South Korea briefly interrupted the production of Korean cars that are sold in the United States. If Korean or other foreign plants were closed for an extended period of time, many American firms would be hurt. A war or other event that would cut trade could have serious consequences for our economy.

Lesson Checkpoint

Text:　Self-Check, text page 379
　　　　Answers

1. Benefits of a positive balance of trade include: greater employment, higher profitability, increased economic growth, larger income for the government to tax, and the ability to buy necessary products from other nations.

2. American firms were less able to raise prices because they were faced with less expensive foreign competition.

3. The practice of selling goods in

foreign markets for less than they are sold in the producing nation is known as *dumping*.

Follow-Up Assignments (Independent Practice/Extension/Homework)

Text: Applying What You Have Learned, text page 379
Answers

One cost, or disadvantage, of buying products from foreign countries involves the loss of employment of U.S. workers due to the increase of imported products; one benefit of such a practice often involves the ability of Americans to purchase comparable—if not superior—quality goods at significantly lower prices. Other answers are acceptable.

Section Evaluation

Self-Check, text page 379
Understanding Economics, questions 4–7 (Chapter 13 Review, text pages 385–387)

SECTION C. The Value of the Dollar and United States Trade (text pages 380–383)

Objectives (Lesson Focus)

Upon completing this section, students will be able to:

- Recognize and describe the importance of the value of the U.S. dollar to our ability to import and/or export products.
- Describe relationships between the value of the U.S. dollar and economic conditions in this country.
- Define the terms appreciation and depreciation.
- Identify and explain factors which caused

the value of the U.S. dollar to appreciate after 1980.
- Identify and explain factors which caused the value of the U.S. dollar to depreciate after 1985.

Preparation (Instruction: Pre-teaching—Vocabulary or Activity)

1. Discussion Introduce this section by asking each student to imagine that they had $15,000 to spend while they were visiting Germany in 1987. Each dollar was worth 1.81 marks on September 1, 1987. Help them figure out how much each of the following items would have cost in dollars at that time. Do this by dividing the price in marks by 1.81. Then figure the same prices at the 1985 exchange rate of 2.84. Discuss how much difference the change in exchange rate made in the apparent price of the products.

	Price in marks	Price in 1987 dollars	Price in 1985 dollars
Volkswagen	15,200	$8,398	$5,352
camera	680	$ 376	$ 239
hotel room	120	$ 66	$ 42
restaurant meal	80	$ 33	$ 21
theater ticket	14	$ 8	$ 5

This difference in price would have made all German products less expensive to Americans in 1985 than they were in 1987. It would also have made U.S. products more expensive to Germans in 1985. Similar situations existed between the United States and most other countries at this time. These facts contributed to our negative balance of trade in 1985.

2. The Personal Narrative The Personal Narrative in Section C describes events surrounding the closing of Mesta Machinery. The subject of the Narrative is a former employee of Mesta. He explains how Mesta's foreign customers in the 1950s and 1960s became their competition in the 1970s and 1980s. Problems related to high wages, doubtful management decisions, and the increased value of the U.S. dollar combined to force the firm to close.

The Narrative emphasizes the importance of exchange rates in determining the ability of American firms to compete internationally. It also describes factors which influence exchange rates, and therefore trade.

Teaching Suggestions (Modeling/Guided Practice)

1. The United States no longer manufactures many products (such as television picture tubes) that we use and import in large quantities from other countries. Point out that if the value of the dollar falls and makes foreign imports more expensive, we will probably pay the higher prices and send even more money out of the country because we no longer have the factories necessary to make these products. This means that a decline in the value of the U.S. dollar may not quickly lead to a reduction in our balance-of-trade problem.

2. Many students do not understand why a firm would sell products to foreign countries for less than they charge customers in their own country (dumping). Tell your students to imagine that they owned a firm in a foreign country. They employ a worker who by law cannot be fired or laid off. They have to pay the worker $100 a day no matter what (many foreign countries have such laws).

    If the worker produced nothing, they would still have to pay him and would therefore lose $100. If he produced goods that could be sold in a foreign nation for $80 (disregarding other costs), they would still lose money, but only $20 a

day. Point out that under these conditions the firm would be much better off selling the product at a loss (dumping) than to pay the worker for doing nothing. This situation roughly explains why firms in some countries are willing to sell goods for less than the goods cost to produce.

Lesson Checkpoint

Text: Self-Check, text page 383
        Answers

1. Exchange rates are set in an international market according to the demand and supply for different types of money.
2. Any event that would change either the supply or demand for a type of money would affect its exchange rate.
3. An appreciation of the U.S. dollar would probably reduce foreign demand for American products.

Follow-up Assignments (Independent Practice/Extension/Homework)

1. Text: Applying What You Have Learned, text page 383
            Answers

    a. The price of Japanese products went up because it took more U.S. dollars to buy the yen needed to purchase these products.
    b. Japanese tourists came to the United States because they could get more dollars for their yen. This made our prices seem lower to them.
    c. The Japanese businesses are either being much more efficient or they are accepting lower profits.

d. Americans may continue to buy Japanese products at higher prices if they believe that their quality is worth the extra price.

2. Teacher's Resource Binder: Critical Thinking Activity, Chapter 13 (answers in Binder).

Section Evaluation

Self-Check, text page 383
Understanding Economics, questions 8 and 9 (Chapter 13 Review, text pages 385–387)

ADDITIONAL MATERIALS FOR CHAPTER 13

Chapter Evaluation

Teacher's Resource Binder: Chapter 13 Quiz

Reteaching and Extension

See the *Teacher's Resource Binder* and the *Student Activity Guide* for additional handouts and activities for Chapter 13.

TEACHER'S BIBLIOGRAPHY FOR CHAPTER 13

Economics Sources

Adams, John. *International Economics: A Self-Teaching Introduction to the Basic Concepts*, 2nd ed. New York: St. Martin's Press, 1979. A programmed self-study book on the most important concepts of international trade and international finance.

Aliber, Robert Z. *The International Money Game.* New York: Basic Books, 1983. A fairly complete treatment of the role of money in international trade and finance.

Basics of Foreign Trade and Exchange. Federal Reserve Bank of New York, 1983. A 16-page booklet that explains the principles of for-

eign trade and exchange with a simplified visual for showing gains through trade.

Edwards, Chris. *The Fragmented World: Competing Perspectives on Trade, Money and Crisis.* New York: Methuen and Co., 1985. Provides a variety of viewpoints on international economics. A good reference.

Olnek, Jay I. *The Invisible Hand: How Free Trade Is Choking the Life out of America.* Greenwich, Conn.: North Stonington Press, 1982. One of the few books that speaks out against free trade.

Stewart, Michael. *The Age of Independence: Economic Policy in a Shrinking World.* Cambridge, Mass.: The M.I.T. Press, 1987. A brief account of the domestic problems that develop as a consequence of our international trade policy.

References for Additional Teaching Strategies

Morton, John, et al. *High School Economics Courses.* New York: Ioint Council on Economic Education, 1985. See Lesson 21, "Why Specialize and Trade?" and Lesson 22, "Foreign Currencies and Foreign Exchange."

Return to Mocha. AMOCO Foundation, 1986. Video Outreach, c/o J.N. Company, P.O. Box 1199, Melville, N.J. 11747. An appealing film in cartoon format that shows how trade develops between and among nations. May send blank tape and it will be copied and returned free along with a teacher's guide.

The Story of Foreign Trade and Exchange. Federal Reserve Bank of New York, 1984. Presents the basic principles of foreign trade and exchange in a 24-page comic book.

Wilde about Trade. Federal Reserve Bank of San Francisco. A 15-minute tape on why nations trade and how foreign exchange rates are determined.

CHAPTER 13 REVIEW ANSWERS

Building Your Vocabulary (text page 386)

1. appreciation
2. depreciation
3. tariff
4. comparative advantage
5. absolute advantage
6. quota
7. protective tariff
8. protection of domestic jobs
9. national security
10. infant industry
11. maintaining economic stability
12. restrictive tariff
13. trade adjustment assistance
14. exchange rate
15. positive balance of trade
16. negative balance of trade
17. dumping
18. revenue tariff

Understanding Economics (text pages 386–387)

1. To follow the theories of absolute and comparative advantage, countries should specialize in producing products that they make most efficiently and trade for the items that they are not able to produce efficiently. This will improve their productivity because they won't be allocating resources to the types of production at which they are least efficient.

2. Countries that are not economically advanced often place high tariffs on imports to increase the price of these imports and to encourage their people to buy products made in their own country.

3. These countries do not want to be dependent on other countries for products they need to defend themselves. They choose to make these products themselves rather than risk a future cut-off in their supply from a foreign country.

4. A country that has a positive balance of trade can expect to have the following advantages:

   a. greater employment
   b. more profitable firms
   c. more growth
   d. a larger tax base

5. The low price of imported goods have benefited all consumers. On the other hand, people who might have produced these products in the United States may have not been able to find work. Thus, the cost of these imported goods is not evenly distributed.

6. People who produce oil in the United States found their income declining with the price of oil in 1985 and 1986.

7. The voluntary limits on the export of cars from Japan increased the price of these cars in the United States and saved over 40,000 jobs in the U.S. auto industry.

8. To say that the value of the dollar appreciated 40 percent means that the dollar could buy 40 percent more units of other types of currency after this happened. Therefore, the price of foreign goods appeared to be lower to U.S. consumers.

9. Three nontrade-related reasons for the appreciation of the U.S. dollar in the early 1980s include:

   a. high interest rate in the U.S. leading foreigners to invest here
   b. instability in other countries leading foreigners to invest here
   c. the early recovery from recession causing foreigners to invest here

Thinking Critically About Economics
(text page 387)

1. Higher tariffs would please workers and businesses that had been hurt by imported goods, however, higher tariffs would displease other people who have to pay higher prices as a result and those who might be hurt by tariffs put on our exports by other countries.

2. Student answers will vary according to their individual points of view. Their answers should be graded relative to the logic on which they are based.

3. If Congress had been able to override President Reagan's veto of the 1985 trade bill, the price of many imported goods would have gone up. This could have resulted in higher prices for domestic goods as well. Although there would have been more jobs in specific industries, there would have been fewer jobs in other industries that depend on these imports. It is possible that other countries could have reacted by increasing their tariffs, which would have hurt U.S. exports.

4. If a country sells products to other countries for less than it sells them to its own people, it could be both creating jobs and reducing unemployment. Dumping would also contribute to a positive balance of trade and of payments.

5. If lower interest rates go down in the United States, foreigners will be less interested in depositing their money in our banks. This would reduce the demand for the dollar as well as reduce its value.

6. Student lists will vary. The basic issue to be determined is whether or not each student would be willing to pay more for a product to provide jobs to other Americans. Their answers may also deal with the question of quality.

Special Skills Projects   (text page 387)

1. It might be interesting to investigate the possibility of a change in the perception that people have of American goods over the past five to ten years. Do people now have a higher or lower opinion of U.S. quality? What might have caused any changes?

2. In early 1987 the value of the U.S. dollar was falling, or depreciating. The result of this trend had not become evident at that time. By the time this text is in use, there should be a clear answer to this question.

CHAPTER 14

Underdeveloped Nations, Population, and Growth (text pages 390–413)

SECTION A.   The Problems of Third World Nations (text pages 393–397)

Objectives   (Lesson Focus)

Upon completion of this section, students will be able to:

- Identify and describe problems that are common to many underdeveloped nations, including traditional economies, a lack of infrastructure, what has been called the "brain drain," and weak political systems.

- Identify and describe different attitudes held by Americans toward extending aid to underdeveloped nations.

Preparation   (Instruction: Pre-teaching— Vocabulary or Activity)

1. Discussion Introduce this section by asking each student to identify one task that requires some basic technical skill that they were taught to do by a parent or guardian. Using a VCR, running a dishwasher, repairing a car, or changing a light bulb would be good examples. List these tasks on the chalkboard.

Tell your students to imagine what their lives would have been like if no one they knew could teach them how to do these things, that they didn't know how to read, and there were no schools. Stress the difficulty of acquiring new knowledge if you have no base of understanding from which to build. The more you know, the easier learning becomes. Emphasize that this problem is common in underdeveloped nations. In such a situation, how much good would it do to send people a new tractor, electric generator, or water pump?

2. The Personal Narrative The Personal Narrative in Section A describes the steps taken by individuals in the United States to help people in Africa. The subject of the Narrative is a young black American woman who becomes aware of starvation and other problems of some countries in Africa from watching television news reports. She wonders why the problems occurred and what she could do to help.

The Narrative shows that although many Americans are willing to give help to underdeveloped nations, we often do not understand the nature of these problems or their causes.

Teaching Suggestions (Modeling/Guided Practice)

1. Ask your students to identify as many examples as possible of infrastructure used by a manufacturing firm in their local area. For each provided example of infrastructure, discuss what different course of action would have been required by the firm in order to continue production had this type of infrastructure not existed in their community. (Students might pose the following example as a basis for discussion: "How could a firm that produces machine tools operate if there were no electric company?") Point out that underdeveloped nations face similar difficulties in efficiently producing goods, since no developed infrastructure is present.

2. Ask your students to pretend that they are twenty-three years old and have just recently graduated with college degrees. They are now offered two different jobs (for ease of discussion, hereafter identified as *Job 1* and *Job 2*). Job 1 is local, thus allowing them to remain close to family and friends. Job 1 requires employees to work 48 hours a week, earning $8,000 annually with few fringe benefits. Furthermore, the firm's equipment is technologically outdated. Job 2, in contrast, would require a lengthy commute from their homes. Employee schedules are based on a 40-hour work week, and workers earn an annual income of $32,000. In addition, extensive fringe benefits are offered by the firm, and workers are provided with quality, up-to-date equipment to aid them in performing their job functions.

Ask your students to choose either Job 1 or Job 2. Point out that this is the type of "choice" encountered by many educated people from underdeveloped nations. They must weigh the costs and benefits carefully. What other costs and benefits can your students suggest that would likely be involved in this decision?

3. Ask your students to identify potential problems that could result from an attempt to form a new country comprised of Alaska, the eastern region of Russia, and Japan. Although these areas are geographically close to one another, their respective people, languages, social values, and economic systems are very different. Governing such a nation would be virtually impossible. Explain that comparable problems often occur in underdeveloped nations that were formerly considered "possessions," or colonies, ruled by other countries. These nations' boundaries were often drawn with little or no consideration for the social, political, or economic values of the people who inhabit them.

Lesson Checkpoint

Text: Self-Check, text page 397
        Answers

  1. Families are virtually the only source of learning in traditional economies.

  2. Many underdeveloped countries have traditional economies, which make it difficult to bring about change. Furthermore, such countries are not affluent enough to educate their people to learn to adjust to such changes in a self-sufficient manner.

  3. *Infrastructure* refers to the physical developments necessary for efficient production and distribution of goods and services; telephones, roads, and sewers are infrastructure examples. Lack of such developments prevent underdeveloped nations from successfully competing with wealthier, more developed nations.

Follow-up Assignments   (Independent Practice/Extension/Homework)

Text: Applying What You Have Learned, text page 397
        Answers

Although the students' answers may vary in wording, they should nevertheless identify the following circumstances—or factors—as the major problems faced by underdeveloped nations:

  1. lack of adequate education for their people

  2. lack of tools or capital needed for production

  3. lack of societal organization, or structure, to help their people bring about change

  4. lack of infrastructure

  5. loss of their most talented, self-motivated people, who typically leave their native land to pursue opportunities in developed nations

Section Evaluation

Self-Check, text page 397
Understanding Economics, questions 1–3 (Chapter 14 Review, text pages 409–411)

SECTION B. The Relationship Between "Have" and "Have Not" Nations (text pages 399–403)

Objectives   (Lesson Focus)

Upon completion of this section, students will be able to:

■ Describe the aid given by the United

States in relation to that given by other developed nations.

- Identify and describe limitations that have frequently been placed on U.S. aid by our government.
- Explain difficulties experienced in deciding what sort of aid to extend that could be best used by underdeveloped nations.

Preparation   (Instruction: Pre-teaching—Vocabulary or Activity)

1. Discussion   Introduce this section by holding a discussion similar to the one in the Personal Narrative. List on the chalkboard the points of view expressed in the Narrative. Then ask the students to explain *their* opinions of each. Can your students think of any other points of view concerning foreign aid? Can a distinction be made between humanitarian considerations and those that are political or economic in nature?

2. The Personal Narrative   The Personal Narrative in Section B presents various points of view on the issue of U.S. extension of aid to underdeveloped nations and further speculates that, if such aid is warranted, the amount and type of aid must still be considered.

The Narrative demonstrates the diversity of public opinion that exists within the United States regarding the issue of foreign aid.

Teaching Suggestions   (Modeling/Guided Practice)

1. Ask your students if they consider it reasonable to expect underdeveloped nations to do what we want them to, or to show gratitude when we send them aid. As an analogy, point out that all—or nearly all—students have received help in one form or another from their par-

ents. Ask students if they always show appreciation to their parents for this assistance, or if they always do what their parents want them to do. If not, have them explain the reasons for their contrary actions.

Now ask your students to share their reactions to this comparison of U.S. assistance to foreign nations to parental aid to children. Do they consider this to be a reasonable comparison? Do countries (*should* they) behave like people? When a United States–aided foreign nation does something we consider undesirable, how and to what degree should our government react?

2. Use Discussion Topic 20 from the *Teacher's Resource Binder* regarding one of the problems with some types of aid to underdeveloped nations. Your students should realize that providing fabric to the underdeveloped nation will destroy its newly developing domestic textile industry. These new firms cannot compete with free goods provided by developed nations. This situation demonstrates the potential problem of giving aid that both benefits and harms the receiving nation.

Lesson Checkpoint

Text: Self-Check, text page 403
Answers

1. Other countries claim that their sacrifices in providing foreign aid have been greater than that of the United States, since these nations have contributed greater per capita aid.

2. *Tied aid* refers to money that must be spent exclusively within the United States.

3. Aid to developing nations must be carefully directed to enable na-

tions to help themselves become more self-sufficient.

Follow-up Assignments   (Independent Practice/Extension/Homework)

1. Text: Applying What You Have Learned, text page 403
   Answers

   Virtually all the views presented in the Personal Narrative were in opposition to the sending of unrestricted U.S. aid to foreign countries. The following four arguments were cited to support this general point of view (although students may provide other equally acceptable responses based on the Narrative):

   a. We should help our own poor people in the United States first.

   b. Much of our aid is wasted or stolen.

   c. We should not send aid to countries that do not support our political point of view.

   d. We should not help countries that have little chance of success.

2. Ask your students to survey their parents or other adult relatives concerning the value of foreign aid. Have students ask each of the following questions and report their findings to the class. Discuss the results of the survey. Can any conclusions be drawn about the kind of people who would or would not want the government to give aid?

   a. Do you feel that your family has enough income to maintain an adequate standard of living?

   b. Do you expect your standard of living to improve, stay about the same, or become worse in the next two years?

   c. Do you, or any person who lives with you, receive support from the government? (social security, unemployment compensation, welfare, food stamps, etc.)

   d. Do you believe government aid to underdeveloped nations is spent effectively?

   e. Do you believe government aid to underdeveloped nations should be increased, remain the same, be reduced, or be completely eliminated?

Section Evaluation

Self-Check, text page 403
Understanding Economics, questions 4 and 5 (Chapter 14 Review, text pages 409–411)

SECTION C.   The Population Explosion (text pages 404–407)

Objective   (Lesson Focus)
Upon completion of this section, students will be able to:

■ Describe problems related to population growth that are faced by many underdeveloped nations.

Preparation   (Instruction: Pre-teaching— Vocabulary or Activity)

1. Discussion   Introduce this section by asking your students how many people are in their families. Since many students will have half-brothers and half-sisters, it may be easier to simply ask them how many people they live with. Ask them to discuss and decide what constitutes a "large" family. They will probably agree that "large" begins with approximately five or six family members. Having established this, ask students to identify several advantages and disadvantages of living in a large family. Many of the disadvantages are likely to be economic, while the advantages will probably be more social in nature.

Discuss how large families provide both advantages and disadvantages for people who live in underdeveloped nations. Why have many people suggested that government social programs would help reduce population growth in underdeveloped nations?

2. The Personal Narrative The Personal Narrative in Section C describes problems that result from overpopulation. The subject of the Narrative is a young man who doesn't understand why people continue to have children they will be unable to support or to care for. He sees reports on the news that show masses of poor people in underdeveloped nations. His reaction is to blame the parents in these countries for having too many children.

The Narrative demonstrates that such a point of view concerning population growth in underdeveloped nations is held by many people.

Teaching Suggestions (Modeling/Guided Practice)

1. Explain that increased food production within some underdeveloped nations has led to increased population growth as well. With an increased food supply, parents are able to provide better nutrition for their children, thus resulting in a decreased child mortality rate. Do your students view this as a favorable or unfavorable result? Ask them to identify other possible results of an increase in food production. Point out that such an

increase—by eliminating the need to import food—would allow the nation to spend its money on machines, job training, and other needed goods and services, which in turn would increase the nation's own production capacity.

2. Discuss the costs of raising a child in the United States. (Be sure to include the cost of an education.) Then compare this cost to that of raising a child in an underdeveloped nation. Your students are likely to assume that there would be less expenses required in the underdeveloped country; point out, however, that this is probably *not* the case. Although Americans may spend a larger quantity of money on their children, the necessary expenses—as a percentage of their overall income—are probably less, particularly if educational costs are included. Many underdeveloped nations do not provide public education. Families in these countries can educate their children only by making great personal sacrifices.

3. The population growth in underdeveloped nations can in part be attributed to an overall increase in people's lifespans. The elderly—whether they live in rich or poor nations—require more care than members of most other age groups. Have students discuss any sacrifices that have been made by their families in order to care for an elderly relative. Ask your students if they think such sacrifices would constitute a greater or lesser problem in developing nations. (Be sure to have them explain the reasons for their responses to this question.)

Re-emphasize the point that the *least* economically advantaged family unit—whose subsistence level is barely adequate—is *most* likely to be adversely affected by one of its own family members who is unable to "pull his own weight."

Lesson Checkpoint

Text: Self-Check, text page 407
   Answers

1. People in underdeveloped nations often desire large families in the anticipation that they will need their offspring to provide economic support when they grow old and unable to work.

2. A reduced mortality rate has resulted in people living longer, thus adding to, rather than helping to eliminate, overpopulation problems.

3. A high birthrate results in more children to provide for and educate. In addition, at least for the first few years of their lives, children do not contribute to the enhancement of the nation's economy through production.

Follow-up Assignments   (Independent Practice/Extension/Homework)

1. Text: Applying What You Have Learned, text page 407
   Answers

   The students' lists of advantages and disadvantages may include other acceptable answers that are not provided here; in addition, the degree of importance placed on these "pro" and "con" factors—to an underdeveloped nation as compared to the United States—may *greatly* vary. The rankings given by each student will in part reflect his or her priorities and values. They should be graded according to the logic presented in supporting their answers.

Advantages of a large family in the United States include

a. *lower income taxes.* In most underdeveloped nations, taxes are less important, since they are not reduced for large families.

b. *more government aid if you are poor.* In an underdeveloped nation such aid is so minimal—if it exists at all—that having extra children would add nothing to a family's standard of living.

c. *more family members to help one another.* This is considered a particularly important asset in a poor, underdeveloped nation, where often the only support offered to the elderly is that provided by their offspring.

Disadvantages of a large family in the United States include

a. *greater overall living expenses in raising a large family.* Increased expenses is an equal—if not greater—problem in many underdeveloped nations, where the most serious overpopulation exists.

b. *lack of ability to provide advanced education for all children.* In many underdeveloped nations, a large family can prevent the children from obtaining *any* education.

c. *inadequate nutrition for all children.* This is a particularly common occurrence in many underdeveloped nations, where the percentage of large families with many children far exceeds such U.S. families.

2. Teacher's Resource Binder: Critical Thinking Activity, Chapter 14 (answers in Binder).

Section Evaluation

Self-Check, text page 407
Understanding Economics, questions 6 and 7 (Chapter 14 Review, text pages 409–411)

ADDITIONAL MATERIALS FOR CHAPTER 14

Chapter Evaluation

Teacher's Resource Binder: Chapter 14 Quiz

Reteaching and Extension

See the *Teacher's Resource Binder* and the *Student Activity Guide* for additional handouts and activities for Chapter 14.

TEACHER'S BIBLIOGRAPHY FOR CHAPTER 14

Economics Sources

External Debt in Perspective. International Monetary Fund, 700 19th Street N.W., Washington, D.C.: 1984. A compilation of articles from the Fund's magazine, *Finance and Management*, on external debts, addresses by the Fund's Managing Director and analytical tables taken from the *1983 World Economic Outlook*.

Finance and Development. A quarterly publication of the International Monetary Fund and the World Bank, Box A-841, Washington, D.C. 20431. Excellent and short articles on economic development with primary focus on the Third World.

Meier, Gerald M. *Emerging from Poverty.* New York: Oxford University Press, 1984. A nontechnical and easy-to-read discussion of current developmental problems.

Todaro, Michael P. *Economic Development in the Third World*, 3rd ed. New York: Longman, 1985. A good reference work for the teacher, particularly on foreign aid and investment.

World Development Report, 1986. New York: Oxford University Press, 1986. Contains articles devoted to many aspects of development as well as a broad range of statistics helpful to researchers.

References for Additional Teaching Strategies

O'Neill, James B., et al. *Strategies for Teaching Economics, World Studies.* New York: Joint Council on Economic Education, 1980. Lesson 7, "Patterns of Economic Development," contains three handouts showing different growth characteristics and Lesson 8, "Less Developed Economies," identifies measurements as well as development institutions such as the World Bank and International Monetary Fund, with eight handouts.

CHAPTER 14 REVIEW ANSWERS

Building Your Vocabulary   (text page 410)

1. matching funds
2. "brain drain"
3. traditional economy
4. mortality rate
5. infrastructure
6. tied aid
7. underdeveloped nations

Understanding Economics (text page 410)

1. In a traditional economic system, people learn how to produce goods and services from their families. There is often no formalized system of education and therefore no established vehicle for introducing new ideas or for bringing about change.

2. A lack of infrastructure increases the costs of production. Without adequate roads, power, and water, it is difficult to produce and transport goods and services efficiently.

3. The boundaries of many underdeveloped nations were established in the 1800s by European colonial powers. The determination of these boundaries, however, often make little social, political, or economic sense. People who do not share a common background, for example, have been forced together into countries and thus frequently find it difficult to govern themselves effectively or fairly.

4. A tool is no more useful than the ability of the person who uses it. Sending tools to people who do not know how to use them will not help these people to become more productive.

5. The two "strings" that have often been put on U.S. aid include the stipulation that the aid must be spent in the United States (tied) and that the receiving country had to put up half of the money needed to support a project (matching funds).

6. Countries with high rates of population growth often have difficulty in achieving economic growth because the additional production they achieve is largely taken up supporting the increased population.

7. Many people in underdeveloped nations value large families for a variety of reasons. To reduce the rate of population growth, it is necessary to either convince them or force them to have fewer children. In either case, these people have to be taught how to limit their family size, a tremendous national reorientation that could only be effective under a well-organized government.

Thinking Critically About Economics
(text pages 410–411)

1. Student lists will vary with their individual family backgrounds.

2. The people in the various countries of Africa are very different from one another. They have different languages, religions, and social systems. To have them join together would be an open invitation to political, social, and economic discord.

3. Opening a factory in any location requires the four factors of production. The needed raw materials might be easily available in the form of trees. A skilled labor force, however, would be very difficult to obtain in the middle of a jungle. The necessary capital, or tools, would also be difficult to build in the middle of a jungle. Finally, managers would be needed to run the factory. Attracting qualified managers to live in a jungle would also be a problem. It would be doubtful that a paper factory could be a success in any jungle, South American or otherwise. (This was in fact attempted in the mid-1970s in Brazil. The project failed.)

4. It is likely that your students will emphasize vocational training. Be careful of attempts to make everyone Ph.D.s. There should be a reasonable chance that

these people would be able to realistically use their education.

5. The aid payments had to be spent in the United States to prevent a flow of dollars out of this country and to provide jobs and business for American workers and firms.

6. Student answers will vary with their personal points of view and values. Their answers should be graded according to the logic used to support them.

7. Any steps that are to be taken must either address the rate of population growth and/or the rate of economic growth. Steps should limit population or increase production.

Special Skills Projects   (text page 411)

1. Your students will probably find that adults are often against sending more aid to underdeveloped nations but are willing to send tools. This probably reflects their desire to see people in underdeveloped nations learn to support themselves.

2. Your students will discover that their neighborhoods are absolutely full of examples of infrastructure. You could try to place some sort of value on these things. Why would it be hard for an underdeveloped nation to compete with firms that exist in a nation that already has a developed infrastructure?

3. Your students will probably find that families are smaller now than they were in the past. Students frequently enjoy discussing why many people have chosen to have fewer children and whether this is a wise choice. What does this show about changing values in this country?

CHAPTER 15

Alternative Economic Systems (text pages 414–435)

SECTION A.   Ownership and Control in Socialism (text pages 416–420)

Objectives   (Lesson Focus)

Upon completion of this section, students will be able to:

- Describe the basic characteristics of a socialist economic system.
- Explain how the basic economic questions *what, how,* and *for whom* are answered in socialist economic systems.
- Describe weaknesses that socialists find in the capitalistic economic system.
- Identify and describe weaknesses capitalists find in socialist economic systems.

Preparation   (Instruction: Pre-teaching— Vocabulary or Activity)

1. Discussion   Introduce this section by describing in general how a socialist economy works. Then ask your students to help you compile a list of all the types of decisions made by businesses in a capitalist economic system. Items that could appear on the list include:

What product to make
Where to produce the product
How to make the product
Who to buy raw materials from
How many workers to hire
How much to pay workers
What price to charge for the product
How to market the product

What equipment to invest in

What to do with left-over funds (profits)

All of these decisions are made by government-planning agencies in a socialist society. Discuss possible reasons why it would be difficult for a planning agency to know what the best, or most efficient, answer to each of these questions would be. Point out that when decisions like these must be made for millions of firms, the chance of making many mistakes is very high.

2. The Personal Narrative The Personal Narrative in Section A describes a young man who lives in the socialist economy of Sweden. He is currently training to become a welder and hopes to be employed in a government-owned shipyard when he completes his training. He is aware of individual advantages and responsibilities that result from the socialist economy in which he lives. Although he believes that he will personally contribute his best effort to production, he is not sure that all other people will do the same.

The Narrative identifies and describes some of the advantages and dangers of a socialist economic system.

Teaching Suggestions (Modeling/Guided Practice)

1. Tell your students the following story:

Imagine that you are all in the same English class. Your teacher announces that there will be a major unit test next week but that it will be graded differently than other tests. The individual scores from each test will be averaged together, and each student will receive the class average for their grade, instead of the score that was placed on their own individual test.

Ask your students if they believe this would be a good plan. Would they study more or less if this were how grades were to be determined?

Point out how this situation relates to production and the distribution of income in a socialist economic system. The individual scores of the students could be regarded as profit. When they are unable to earn any "profit" (their own individual score), they may have less incentive to work hard.

2. Remind your students that there are many characteristics of socialism that can be found in the mixed American economy. One example is our Social Security system. Discuss the reasons for its establishment in 1935. Are these reasons as valid today as they were during the Great Depression? What would be the costs and benefits of eliminating the Social Security system? Would people who paid the costs be the same as those who would receive the benefits?

What other characteristics of socialism can be found in the U.S. economy? Possible characteristics of socialism include the U.S. Postal Service, progressive income taxes, welfare, unemployment compensation, public schools, and the Medicare and Medicaid systems.

3. Point out the fact that many Americans are wealthy only because their parents or other relatives were financially successful and left them money when they died. Do your students believe this is fair? Some people have suggested that estates should be heavily taxed so that people would have a more equalized start, or chance at being successful. Discuss this idea with your students. To what extent is the knowledge that you can leave your wealth to your children an incentive to work hard? Would older people waste their money and wealth if they thought the government would take it when they died?

Lesson Checkpoint

Text: Self-Check, text page 420

Answers

1. In socialism, the government has control over the basic economic questions *what* and *how*, and substantial control over *for whom*.

2. Socialists assert that their system provides a more equitable distribution of income and wealth.

3. Within the socialist system, the provision of a basic standard of living and the taxing of higher incomes may be contributing factors in the lessened incentive to work hard.

Follow-up Assignments   (Independent Practice/Extension/Homework)

1. Text: Applying What You Have Learned, text page 420

   Answers

   (1) The following five answers may be cited by students to illustrate how Sven's life within a socialist country differs from their own lives in our capitalist country:

   a. Many of the firms that Sven could have considered as his potential employers are owned and run by the Swedish government itself.

   b. Even if they lose rather than earn a profit, many of these businesses continue to operate.

   c. The taxes Sven will pay when he goes back to work are much higher than he would be required to pay in the United States.

   d. The Swedish government will provide Sven with much greater, more extensive benefit programs, such as free medical care.

   e. It would be difficult for Sven to lose a job, whether or not he works hard.

   (2) Most students will probably agree with the assertion that "People work best for their own personal gain." You might choose to extend this concept a bit farther by asking your students if they think such a motivator is a "learned" characteristic or simply an intrinsic part of human nature.

2. Teacher's Resource Binder: Critical Thinking Activity, Chapter 15 (answers in Binder).

Section Evaluation

Self-Check, text page 420
Understanding Economics, questions 1–4 (Chapter 15 Review, text pages 432–434)

SECTION B.   Ownership and Control of Resources in Communism (text pages 421–425)

Objectives   (Lesson Focus)

Upon completion of this section, students will be able to:

- Describe the basic characteristics of communism.

- Explain similarities to and differences between socialism and communism.

- Describe basic ideas of Karl Marx, including his concepts of the dictatorship of the proletariat and the withering away of the state.
- Identify and describe economic problems of the Soviet Union's economic and political system.

Preparation   (Instruction: Pre-teaching—Vocabulary or Activity)

1. Discussion   Two possible courses of action—presented in the form of alternatives—are offered for each of the following numbered entries. Each question is intended to stimulate thinking in regard to the advantages and disadvantages among alternative economic systems and the involvement of trade-offs within these systems. Keeping these objectives in mind, introduce this section by asking your students to choose one of the alternatives presented for each entry. Then discuss differing student choices with the class as a whole.

Question: Which is more important to you?

a. being able to choose from a limited selection of clothing types at lower prices *or* being able to choose from a variety of clothing types at higher prices

b. being guaranteed a job by the government *or* being able to start up your own business if you so desire

c. being assured of a minimum standard of living *or* being paid according to the value of what you are able to produce

d. paying lower prices that result in frequent shortages for many necessary products *or* paying higher prices but usually having the products available

e. having the government guarantee a minimum standard of living for everyone, with no potential available for becoming wealthy *or* having no restrictions placed on—or guarantees added to—the standard of living, thus allowing both for wealth and poverty

f. having free higher education provided for those who qualify on a test *or* being able to attend college only if you are able to pay for your own education

g. being provided with free medical care, but little if any personal choice in the selection of a doctor *or* paying your own medical expenses to the doctor of your choice

Explain that all of these questions involve trade-offs that are similar to those made between advantages offered by pure command and pure market economies. The first alternative in each case is associated with a command economy and offers a degree of personal security in exchange for some economic freedom. The second alternative is commonly found in capitalism and offers more economic freedom but less personal security. Discuss the choices your students make. Do they place more value on personal security or on economic freedom? Point out that this listing only compares economic differences, not political ones, between systems.

2. The Personal Narrative   The Personal Narrative in Section B describes the life of a Russian student who currently lives with his aunt and uncle just outside of Moscow. Misha, the subject of the Narrative, had made favorable test scores and was thus accepted at the government-run school to pursue his chemistry studies. Because of his uncle's job status as a factory foreman, the three family members are able to live quite comfortably—at least by Russian standards—in a large apartment. The Narrative describes the contributions made by each individual to the family unit and explains both the economic advantages they enjoy and the problems they must overcome.

The Narrative demonstrates some of the differences between trade-offs that have been made in the Soviet economy and those that have occurred in the United States.

Teaching Suggestions (Modeling/Guided Practice)

1. Find a newspaper article that discusses a local firm that has recently gone out of business. Discuss the circumstances under which this occurred. Then ask your students to predict what would have happened if the same firm had existed in the Soviet economy. Would it have gone out of business? What does this tell your students about the efficiency of allocation of resources in centrally planned economic systems? How can you judge the efficiency or success of a firm if it is not intended to earn a profit? The successful adherence to government plans does not in and of itself guarantee that the plans had initially set appropriate objectives for the firm. Firms could be quite inefficient and wasteful yet still meet the designated plans.

2. Use Discussion Topic 21 from the *Teacher's Resource Binder* to illustrate one of the problems with incentive in a socialist economy.

   Your students should recognize that Peter would have less incentive to build the machine, because he would receive little personal reward and could certainly cause problems by causing 50 workers to lose their jobs.

Lesson Checkpoint

Text:　Self-Check, text page 425
　　　Answers

　　1. Marx maintains that the sole aim of capitalists is to earn profit.

2. While socialists defend the role of the individual within the political process, communists grant political power to a small group only, who create and enforce rules for the rest of society.

3. Rigid government control in the Soviet Union has hindered its economy through the production of inferior products and the misallocation of many resources.

Follow-up Assignments (Independent Practice/Extension/Homework)

Text:　Applying What You Have Learned, text page 425
　　　Answers

Differences in Misha's life within a communist society include:

1. His higher education is free.
2. The prices he pays for products do not reflect their costs of production.
3. Medical care in the Soviet Union is paid for by the government.
4. There are shortages of many basic consumer items.
5. There is little or no inflation in the Soviet economy.

Section Evaluation

Self-Check, text page 425
Understanding Economics, questions 5–7 (Chapter 15 Review, text pages 432–434)

SECTION C.　Ownership and Control of Resources in Market Socialism (text pages 427–430)

Objectives (Lesson Focus)

Upon completion of this section, students will be able to:

- Describe the basic characteristics of market socialism.

- Describe several economic accomplishments and problems of market socialism as it is practiced in Yugoslavia.

- Draw and explain general conclusions concerning the advantages and disadvantages of the major economic systems: capitalism, socialism, communism, and market socialism.

Preparation　(Instruction: Pre-teaching—Vocabulary or Activity)

1. Discussion　Introduce this section by asking students to list the characteristics, or qualities, that would make a person an efficient manager. Then they should make a second list of characteristics that would make a person a popular manager. Discuss differences between the two lists.

Tell your students to imagine that they were in charge of an enterprise in Yugoslavia that was losing money. They are convinced that one of the following three actions will have to be taken. Ask your students which action they would choose and to explain why they would choose it. What problems could each of these choices result in for the entire economy?

a. Reduce wage rates by 10 percent

b. Increase prices by 10 percent

c. Lay off 10 percent of the workers

2. The Personal Narrative　The Personal Narrative in Section C describes the problems of one family that lives under market socialism in Yugoslavia. The subject of the Narrative is a young man whose father is an elected manager of a firm. He is responsible for making economic decisions that will maintain his firm's competitive position within a market economy. At the same time, he must remain popular with the workers who elected him.

The Narrative shows the conflict between these two sets of objectives. Decisions that will maintain his popularity with the workers may be economically unwise.

The Narrative demonstrates the characteristics of socialism and capitalism that are combined to form market socialism. It shows that achieving all the objectives of this system may be difficult if not impossible.

Teaching Suggestions　(Modeling/Guided Practice)

1. Point out that working hard in the Yugoslav economy will not provide an individual with a much higher income. The individual's firm and the people who work for that firm might benefit, but the individual will not become personally wealthy. Discuss why many economists believe that market socialism also suffers from a lack of personal incentive. Would any of your students stay up all night working to earn another $100 if they knew they would have to share it with all the other students in their class?

2. Explain that most basic investment decisions in Yugoslavia are made by the government and may be based on political as well as economic considerations. For example, more industrial investments have been made in the northern part of the country than in the southern part. This has tended to create more industrial jobs that pay higher wages in the north. Some people have suggested that this has happened because Northerners hold greater political power within the government. Whether this accusation is true or not, it shows that eliminating private ownership of the means of production does not guarantee equality.

3. Ask your students what kind of person they would elect to be principal of their

school if they were given the power to do so. Would they choose a principal who would be able to create conditions that were necessary to achieve a quality education? Why would principals chosen in this way find it difficult to do their jobs? In what ways would this situation be similar to the situation found in the Yugoslav economy where workers choose their managers?

Lesson Checkpoint

Text: Self-Check, text page 430
      Answers

1. Characteristics of socialism found in market socialism include: high taxes; extensive social benefits; and government ownership of means of production. Characteristics of capitalism include: resources allocated according to market forces; prices set in competitive market; and wages determined according to value of labor.
2. To a capitalist, "residue" is considered to be profit.
3. Since managers in market socialism are elected by the workers themselves, they must be more sensitive to worker demands in order to maintain their positions.

Follow-up Assignments   (Independent Practice/Extension/Homework)

Text: Applying What You Have Learned, text page 430
      Answers

Workers' councils in Yugoslavia and the owners of capitalistic firms in the United States both must:

1. decide what raw materials to buy
2. set prices

3. set wages
4. hire or appoint the managers who make the day-to-day decision in running the firm

Workers' councils would have to take the following actions that the owners of capitalistic firms would not have to take:

1. allocate housing
2. campaign to be elected manager
3. risk being taken over by the government if they don't earn a profit

Section Evaluation

Self-Check, text page 430
Understanding Economics, questions 8 and 9 (Chapter 15 Review, text pages 432–434)

ADDITIONAL MATERIALS FOR CHAPTER 15

Chapter Evaluation

Teacher's Resource Binder: Chapter 15 Quiz

Reteaching and Extension

See the *Teacher's Resource Binder* and the *Student Activity Guide* for additional handouts and activities for Chapter 15.

TEACHER'S BIBLIOGRAPHY FOR CHAPTER 15

Economics Sources

Ebenstein, William, and Fogelman, Edwin. *Today's Isms: Communism, Fascism, Capitalism and Socialism.* 9th ed. Englewood Cliffs, N.J.: 1985. A very popular and easy to read book that explores the "isms" from both political science and economic systems points of view. Can be used by the above-average student.

Haitani, Kanji. *Comparative Economic Systems:*

Organizational and Managerial Perspectives. Englewood Cliffs, N.J.: Prentice-Hall, 1986. Analyzes the three most influential economies: the United States, the Soviet Union, and the Japanese. Discussion includes social, cultural, and political as well as economic differences. References are made to other economies.

Lechechman, Robert, and Van Loon, Borin. *Capitalism for Beginners.* New York: Pantheon Books, 1981. A pre- and post-Keynesian look at capitalism with comparisons to Marxism. Lively reading.

Miller, James R. *The ABCs of Soviet Socialism.* Urbana, IL: University of Illinois Press, 1981. Analyzes the historical, political, and economic performance of the Soviet Union.

Prout, Christopher. *Market Socialism in Yugoslavia.* Oxford: Oxford University Press, 1985. Examines the evolution of market socialism in Yugoslavia.

Schneitzer, Martin C., and Nordyke, James W. *Comparative Economic Systems*, 3rd ed. Cincinnati: South-Western Publishing Co., 1983. A simple elementary college text with chapters devoted to different countries.

CHAPTER 15 REVIEW ANSWERS

Building Your Vocabulary   (text page 433)

1. dictatorship of the proletariat
2. market socialism
3. workers' councils
4. incentive
5. socialism
6. communism
7. withering away of the state
8. decentralized

Understanding Economics   (text page 433)

1. People who believe in alternative economic systems often believe that profit results in a misallocation of resources. They claim that goods and services are provided for people who are wealthy and that few resources are used to satisfy the needs of ordinary people.

2. Socialists believe that competition is wasteful because it can cause too many goods of the same type to be produced. They suggest that this results in a waste of capital that could be better used for other types of production.

3. Both socialist and communist systems are slow to change because they are controlled by a government agency. Such organizations rely on rules and are often hesitant to change them to adapt to new economic conditions.

4. Socialistic and communistic firms are not run to earn a profit. It is therefore difficult to judge their efficiency. Meeting a government plan does not necessarily prove that resources are being used efficiently.

5. Socialism values individual freedom. It seeks the participation of the people in making social and economic decisions through a political process. Communism is based on the belief that personal freedom and ownership of the means of production would be used by some people to take advantage of other people. It therefore relies on decisions made through a totalitarian form of government.

6. Karl Marx believed that freedom of choice would lead some people to take advantage of other people. He stated that to create socialism people would have to be forced to share and cooperate by a totalitarian form of government.

7. There are parts of both the Soviet and

the Swedish economies that are not socialistic. In Sweden, small firms are allowed to be owned and run by private people. In the Soviet Union, farmers are allowed to grow food to sell it for profit on small plots of land.

8. "Good" managers in an economic sense may not be popular managers with the workers. Therefore, it is difficult for good managers to be elected to workers' councils in Yugoslavia.

9. The high rates of inflation in Yugoslavia may be the result of managers giving workers raises so that they will be re-elected to workers' councils.

Thinking Critically About Economics
(text pages 433–434)

1. Student answers will vary but should be based on logic and supported with the knowledge they have gained in this course.

2. Most of the student questions will probably concern the limitations on political, social, or economic rights in the Soviet Union.

3. Possible reasons for running one's own business in the United States would include:

   a. the desire to earn a profit
   b. the desire to be your own boss
   c. the desire to have something to leave to your children
   d. the desire to build or do something that you can be proud of as an individual

   (Most students will rank earning a profit as most important.)

4. A firm that made inferior products in the United States would soon go out of business because no one would buy them. A similar firm in the Soviet economy could continue to run for many years because individual firms are not responsible for selling their own products and no alternative ones may exist.

5. *People in the Soviet Union give up:*

   a. the right to run their own businesses
   b. the right to own many forms of private property
   c. the chance to become wealthy
   d. the right to participate in many types of economic decisions

   People in the Soviet Union gain:

   a. by not having much inflation
   b. by having little unemployment
   c. by having low prices for basic consumer goods
   d. by having medical care provided by their government

6. Managers in market socialism must not only attempt to keep their workers happy but also ensure that their firm earns a profit. It is often difficult to make decisions that will accomplish both of these goals.

Special Skills Projects   (text page 434)

1. Your students will probably find that many adults do not understand the difference between socialism and communism. You might discuss why this general lack of knowledge exists in the United States.

2. In the past, the Soviet Embassy has been willing to send out large volumes of printed material to American students. Most of the literature will present a very positive view of the security and lack of

economic hardships that the Soviet people enjoy. You may want to discuss other points of view on life in the Soviet Union.

PART 4 REVIEW ANSWERS

Understanding Economic Concepts

1. The answer is provided as an example in the text.

2. The two types of barriers to trade are *tariffs* and *quotas*. A tariff is a tax on imported goods that makes them more expensive and reduces the quantity demanded. A quota is an upper limit on the quantity of a product that may be imported.

3. According to the *infant industry argument*, developing nations should establish tariffs to protect their developing industries from competition from more developed industries in other countries.

4. According to the *national security argument*, countries should produce products that are important to their security even when these products could be purchased at lower cost from other nations. This policy will prevent the supply of these products from being cut off in times of war.

5. Countries would rather have a *positive balance of trade* because they are more likely to have full employment, economic growth, and a larger tax base if they do.

6. One of the most important reasons for the U.S. negative balance of trade in the early 1980s was the high *exchange rate* for the U.S. dollar. Many foreigners found that they had to trade in too many of their units of money to get the dollars they needed to buy American products. It was less expensive for them to buy the products they needed from other countries.

7. Many underdeveloped countries have *traditional economies*, in which most people learn what they know and their values from their families. These countries usually have no developed educational system. This makes it difficult for them to bring about change.

8. Many underdeveloped countries lack basic *infrastructure*, the capital improvements such as roads and electric power necessary to allow their industries to produce goods efficiently. This lack makes it difficult for them to compete with industries in more developed nations that have an advanced infrastructure.

9. Just sending tools and other types of capital to underdeveloped countries usually does little good because the people in these nations often do not know how to use them. Because of the *inadequate education systems* that exist in many of these countries, the capital may well be wasted.

10. A large part of U.S. foreign aid has been *tied* and given in the form of *matching funds*. Tied aid must be spent in this country. Matching funds require the receiving nation to put up half the money for a project. This means that truly poor nations may not be able to take advantage of all the aid that is offered because they cannot afford to match the aid.

11. Advances in medical care have reduced the *mortality rates* in many underdeveloped nations. This has frequently increased the population growth rates in these countries.

12. In both *socialism* and in *communism* the

means of production are owned and controlled by the government. However, socialism allows many political and individual freedoms, while communism relies on a totalitarian form of government, leaving individuals few political or economic choices. In *market socialism* the means of production are also owned by the government, but they are generally controlled by groups of workers. Market socialism relies on the free market to make many economic decisions.

13. People who believe in the socialist economic system argue that socialism provides greater *economic stability* and more equitable *social benefits* than capitalism because most of the basic economic decisions of *What, How,* and *For Whom* are made by the government.

14. People who do not support socialism often argue that socialism suffers from a *lack of worker incentive* and *inflexible control of production* because the government makes most of the basic economic decisions of *What, How,* and *For Whom.*

15. The most significant differences between socialism and communism are political. Socialism prizes individual freedom and political participation, while communism is based on the belief that personal freedom would only be used by some people to exploit others.

16. Market socialism attempts to combine the best aspects of *socialism* and *capitalism*. Under this system, private ownership of the means of production is not allowed. This prevents the private accumulation of wealth. However, the workers of each firm control production and must operate in a competitive market. This is intended to provide them with an incentive to produce quality products and sell them at competitive prices.

Writing About Economics

1. Students' answers should reflect an understanding of the issues involved in each of the identified terms. Their questions on the *protecting domestic jobs* argument should demonstrate an awareness of the trade-offs lower tariffs would bring in the job market. Their questions on *dumping* should show that they understand why industries might choose to sell products below the price they charge customers in their own country. Their questions on the *negative balance of trade* should demonstrate their understanding of the economic impact of a negative balance of trade.

2. Students should understand the fluctuations in the *exchange rates* for the U.S. dollar that took place in the 1980s. Their letters should include a description of various factors that caused the dollar to first increase and then to decrease in value. They should also explain how these changes resulted in increased prices for foreign products that were purchased with U.S. dollars after 1985.

3. Students should understand the problems in achieving economic growth in underdeveloped nations, which result from the *traditional economic systems* and inadequate *infrastructures* that often exist in these countries.

4. Students should understand the three important differences they have chosen to write about. They should demonstrate a knowledge of how the question or problem is answered in each economic system and why the difference is significant.

Discussing Economics

1. Students should identify the issue(s) that are related to the proposed legislation to

require all products sold in the United States to be made at least 80 percent from parts made in this country. Students should clearly state whether or not they support the proposed legislation; they should also clearly explain the costs and benefits associated with the legislation and why they believe their answer is best.

2. Students should identify the issue(s) that are related to placing large tariffs on imported oil and should clearly state whether or not they support such tariffs. Students should clearly explain the costs and benefits associated with the legislation and why they believe their answer is best.

3. Students should identify the issue(s) that are related to American investment in the Soviet Union and should clearly state whether or not they would support such investment. Students should clearly explain the costs and benefits of American investment in the Soviet Union and why they believe their answer is best.

Problem-Solving with Economics

Chapter 13

1. Student answers will vary according to their individual values and points of view. Their explanations should show that they have logically considered issues such as price, quality, and buying American products to help the domestic economy.

2. a. Quotas on imports could increase employment in industries that produce the product, but could also lead to inflation or retaliatory trade barriers by countries that export the product.

   b. Large tariffs could increase employment in industries that produce the product, but could lead to inflation or retaliatory trade barriers by countries that export the product.

   c. Paying unemployment compensation for longer periods of time could help people who are hurt by imports, but could also result in higher taxes and costs of production for other U.S. firms.

   d. Providing government retraining programs for all workers who lose their jobs due to imports would help these workers, but could result in higher taxes and costs of production for other U.S. firms.

   e. Providing government jobs for all workers who lose their jobs due to imports would help these workers, but would increase government spending and probably increase taxes, which would increase the costs of production for other U.S. firms.

Chapter 14

1. Student answers will vary according to their individual points of view. However, all answers should reflect an understanding of the multiple problems faced by underdeveloped nations. Programs that deal with just one aspect are not likely to succeed.

2. Student answers will vary according to their individual points of view.

   a. An increase in U.S. taxes to support additional aid would only help to the extent that the aid was spent on factors that would increase the productivity of underdeveloped economies.

   b. Bringing foreign students to the United States would only help if they returned to their homes and had the tools and other factors of production they needed to increase the productivity of their country's economic system.

c. Building factories in underdeveloped nations would only help if people were trained to work in the factories and there was a market for the goods they produced.

d. Sending U.S. citizens to underdeveloped nations would only help if they had the tools and other capital necessary to increase the underdeveloped nation's productivity.

e. Any other suggestions by students should demonstrate their logical consideration of the problems faced by underdeveloped nations.

3. Students' answers will vary according to their individual values and points of view. Their answers should demonstrate careful consideration of the conflicting values and points of view concerning the issue of limiting population growth.

Chapter 15

1. Students' answers will vary, but should all demonstrate a knowledge of the significant differences between the way in which basic economic decisions are made in the Soviet Union and in the United States. Getting ahead in the Soviet Union has more to do with "fitting in" than with a demonstration of individual initiative. The reverse is often true in the U.S. economic system.

2. Student answers should demonstrate an awareness of the different types of personal characteristics that make individuals good managers or electable leaders. They should make it clear that they understand the inherent contradiction between these characteristics and why this contradiction may make it difficult for a manager in Yugoslavia to run a firm efficiently and still maintain a leadership position over time.